over the Hump :
airlift to China

D1742457

over the Hump: airlift to China
William J Koenig

Pan/Ballantine

Editor-in-Chief: Barrie Pitt
Editor: David Mason
Art Director: Sarah Kingham
Picture Editor: Robert Hunt
Consultant Art Editor: Denis Piper
Designer: John Watson
Illustration: John Batchelor
Photographic Research: Carina Dvorak
Cartographer: Richard Natkiel

ISBN 345 09770 X
First Published in Great Britain 1972 by Pan/Ballantine, London.
Printed by Van Boekhoven-Bosch, Utrecht, Holland.
Ballantine Books, Ltd.
Pan Books, Ltd.
33 Tothill Street, London, SW1.

Contents

China's lifeline

Introduction by S L Mayer

The airlift into China was an integral chapter in the drama of the Pacific War. Its irony lies in the fact that although the military effect was ultimately successful, its political purposes, ill-conceived and hardly planned at all, were devastating in their ultimate failure. This often proves to be the case in operations, military or otherwise, in which planning is made largely on an *ad hoc* basis.

The United States was a most reluctant ally of the British until the attack on Pearl Harbor; Britain, of course, had more pressing problems than the China-Burma-India theatre on its mind in 1940. As a result, the political holding operation which the British were forced to maintain against Japan, a process begun in the early 1920s with the Washington Conference, became the least successful military holding operation of the early months of the Pacific War. True, America could now openly aid the cause, but the loss of insular South-east Asia in

the first four months of the war forced them back to Midway, only a short hop from Hawaii, and most of the American fleet in the Pacific was destroyed in the first hours of the war. So for a long time afterwards the United States was unable to do much about protecting Britain's Indian Empire – even had it wished to do so. President Roosevelt placed the defeat of Hitler's Germany at the top of his priority list and Churchill, naturally enough, agreed with this plan. At the bottom of this same list was the so-called CBI theatre. When Burma quickly fell to Japan along with the rest of South-east Asia, Nationalist China was isolated in its Chungking stronghold. The American-led operations of flying supplies to Chiang Kai-shek over the hump from India helped keep China in the war and, more importantly, tied up a considerable number of Japanese troops in China which could have been used elsewhere. Therefore Roosevelt had to encourage the maintenance of the hump airlift despite the fact that there were not even enough planes to defend the American West Coast if it were attacked in the spring of 1942.

Holding the fort for the Allies in Chungking was 'Vinegar Joe' Stilwell, whose antipathy for the Generalissimo was matched only by the disdain which Chiang felt for Stilwell and his rough but brutally honest and argumentative manner. Roosevelt realised that Chiang was very reluctantly fighting the Japanese, but he also saw what Stilwell did not: that the mere presence of Chiang, with all his corruption, was important in and of itself. The support operations carried out by the British in Burma in 1944-45, and the clearing of Burma by the Allies, were a part of the overall military strategy of keeping Japanese forces tied down in China so that the war could be won by the island-hopping operations in the Pacific. Throughout the war Roosevelt played an ambivalent role. On the one hand he knew that abandoning Chiang and the British in India would serve only to prolong the war and antagonize America's vital ally. On the other hand, Chiang's dictatorial and thoroughly corrupt régime was wasting millions of American dollars and supplies by not taking on the Japanese in a forthright manner, and the Kuomintang in Chungking was hardly a testimony to the ideals of democracy, as embodied in the Atlantic Charter, for which the Allies were presumably fighting. The maintenance of British rule in India and Burma, furthermore, for which Churchill waxed eloquent, was anathema to Roosevelt, who thought that the British, at least under Churchill, had no intention whatever of allowing Britain's subject races to enjoy the benefits of independence and national self-determination after the war was over. So Roosevelt, ignorant of even the geography of China and Southeast Asia, waffled. He neither gave the British in India nor the Nationalist Chinese what they wanted, and although the operations over the hump were a tactical success, the United States, in spite of itself continued to back the Nationalists after the war, even though the old China hands had repeatedly warned the American government that, in Chinese eyes, Chiang had lost the 'mandate of heaven' long before. The victory of the British Labour Party in 1945 at least relieved the United States of the odious task of attempting to force the British to quit India.

William Koenig tells the story of the dangerous flights over the hump and the courage of the men who took the risks which kept Nationalist China alive. There is no question that had these flights not been maintained, China would have fallen to Japan by default and the war in the Pacific would not have been won as quickly as it was. With China out of the war hundreds of thousands of Japanese troops would have been made available for action elsewhere. So the flights were continued, China did not fight, and American pilots risked their lives to give Chiang Kai-shek a second chance in 1945. Chiang's opportunity was wasted. It was a foregone conclusion that this would be the case. And a Nationalist régime, reluctant to fight Japan, was forced to submit to the Communists of Mao Tse-Tung in the four-year Chinese Civil War which followed on the heels of the victory over Japan. But the Americans were stuck with the Nationalists, unwilling to commit themselves to give all-out support to Chiang, but equally unwilling to drop their erstwhile reluctant ally. Roosevelt's attitude was matched by Truman's equal reluctance to give wholehearted support to Chiang. It is tragic that the forthrightness and determination of the pilots who flew the hump was not equalled by their political masters. There was nothing at all ambivalent about their flying over-aged aircraft over the highest mountains in the world.

China is isolated

Chinese troops at the Great Wall of
China prepare to resist the Japanese
advance

The story of the 'Hump' is in reality two stories. On one level, it is the story of Japan's blockade of China and China's resulting isolation, and of American efforts to break that blockade and keep China in the war. On another level, it is the story of the men, the planes, the logistics, and the management and command problems of the largest and most successful air transport operation of the war, an operation in which the transport squadrons flying the hump between China and India lost as many planes as did the combat squadrons of the US Fourteenth Air Force in China. The last link in the longest supply line in the war, the air route from India to China represented China's only line of communication and supply with its allies for three years.

Although Japan had occupied Manchuria in 1931, the Second World War in the Far East is generally considered to have begun on 7th July, 1937 with an incident staged by Japanese forces against the Chinese garrison at the town of Wanping at the eastern end of the Marco Polo Bridge in north China. Wanping was chosen because it lay at the western end of a short railroad connecting the Peking-Tientsin railroad with the important Peking-Hankow line which linked Peking with central China and the national capital at Nanking. Control of this traverse line would enable the Japanese to isolate Peking from the rest of China. The incident was staged to force a withdrawal of Chinese troops from the area. The ultimate aim of the Japanese army was to detach north China from the control of Chiang Kai-shek's Nationalist government at Nanking and establish a 'puppet' state in the same fashion as Manchukuo had been formed in Manchuria in 1932.

In the negotiations following the Marco Polo Bridge incident, the Chinese government under Chiang Kai-shek expressed itself willing to make economic and other concessions but not to give up control of north China. During the negotiations, Japanese troops attacked and destroyed the Chinese forces near Peking and occupied the Peking-Tientsin area. China appealed to the signatories of the Nine Power Treaty of 1922 and to the League of Nations but received no satisfaction whatsoever. With its historic northern capital in Japanese hands and fighting beginning to spread to other areas, China had no alternative but to go to war to protect its territorial integrity.

The Japanese army expected a quick and easy victory. When informing the Emperor of the war, the Chief of the General Staff, General Hajime Sugiyama, predicted the war would be over in a month. But he was not reckoning with the fact that the national crisis in China was causing a general political strengthening of the central government as the communists and other dissident political and military groups came to the support of the Nanking government. Thus China

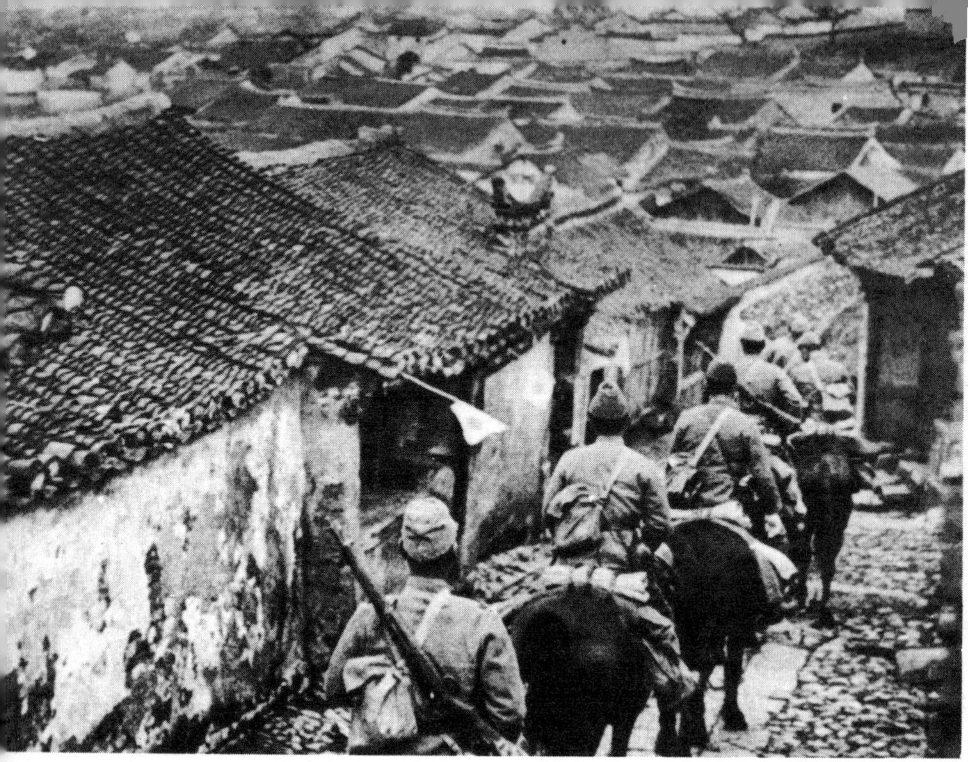

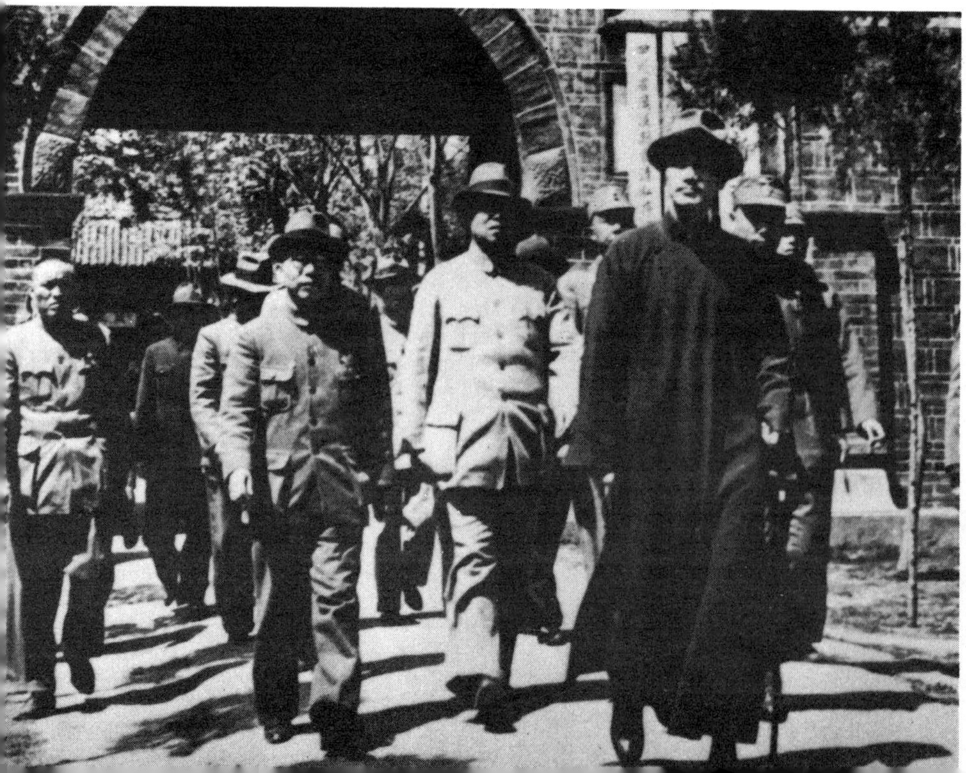

Left: Japanese cavalry enter a Manchurian village in 1931. *Below left:* Wearing a *paozi,* Chiang Kai-shek enters the government building in Canton with his staff. *Below right:* A Japanese artillery unit carries its dismantled mountain guns up a hill during the advance on Peking. *Right:* General Hajime Sugiyama. He told the emperor that the war would be over within one month

Chinese infantry fire on the enemy during the retreat inland

was able to enter the war with a large measure of political unity.

Unable either to accept Japanese demands or to obtain any international pressure against Japan to China's advantage, Chiang Kai-shek prepared to fight a protracted war against Japan. If a quick Japanese victory could be prevented, he believed that the international situation would in time turn more in China's favor and bring the assistance so desperately needed in the forthcoming struggle. In the meantime, Chiang put into effect his already established concept of the geographic needs of protracted war against Japan. As early as 1935 he had written: 'To fight the Japanese, the main battle front should be located in the area south of the Yangtze river and west of the Peking-Hankow Railroad; Loyang, Siangyang-Fancheng, Kingmen-Ichang, and Changteh should constitute the last line of defense. The three provinces of Szechuan, Kweichow, and Shensi would form the nucleus and the provinces of Kansu and Yunnan the rear areas.' Chiang's strategy called for a slow retreat to the mountainous areas of inland China, leaving the less defensible lowlands and coastal areas to the Japanese. He hoped to counter the technical superiority of the Japanese with space by using the great distances of China to force the enemy to overextend his lines of communication and spread his forces. The Chinese could then attack the exposed lines of communication and carry on guerrilla warfare in which space and time would help to wear down enemy strength.

By November 1938 the Japanese offensive had given them control of the Peking-Tientsin area in the north, the Canton area in the south, Hankow and part of central China, and the Shanghai-Nanking area in the east. The largest cities, the key areas in eleven provinces, the three main rivers, ninety-five per cent of the industry, and fifty per cent of the population of China were in the hands of the Japanese. But the battle strategy on which the Japanese commanders had relied to bring a quick end to the war had failed. The plan had been to trap the main Chinese armies in the coastal areas and destroy them, thus ending China's ability to resist. Even though Chiang had delayed his general retreat too long after the magnificent Chinese defense of Shanghai in late 1937 and as a result lost most of his equipment and many troops, the bulk of his forces had still managed to break out of the Japanese trap and escape to the interior.

Although he had to sacrifice his best troops and virtually all his equipment, Chiang's tactic of slow retreat to the interior was basically successful. He and his people had also clearly demonstrated their will to resist in such battles as Taierchuang, Chengchow and, most importantly, the three-month siege of Shanghai in which the attacking Japanese lost 40,000 troops and the defending Chinese 250,000. The Chinese government was now established in the mountain city of Chungking in the western province of Yunnan. The Japanese were not able to penetrate the river gorges and mountain passes which formed the basis of Chiang's inland defenses while he in turn was unable to challenge the Japanese forces in the lowlands. The conflict thus turned into a military stalemate and war of attrition. From 1938 until 1945 little territory changed hands.

From this point, China's ability to maintain any kind of a war effort became almost entirely a question of supply. Even before the war, China's own productive capacities were modest. In 1936 the production of pig iron was a paltry 870,000 tons while the production of another vital necessity of war – petroleum – was measured only in hundreds of pounds per day. China was able to produce some light arms of good quality but no heavy war equipment such as trucks, tanks, artillery, or planes. Throughout the war, even basic items such as rifle bullets were never in plentiful supply. With the onset of full scale hostilities, the Chinese government made a

Japanese tanks mass to enter Nanking after the city has been bombarded

supreme effort to save what industrial plant it had by relocating it in safer inland areas. By January 1939 some 300 factories had been moved to the interior. The defense of Shanghai was a calculated move in this effort but the machinery saved in the evacuation was dearly bought and perhaps not worth the vast amount of equipment and first line troops lost. China now had to pay the price for its past policy of sacrificing basic industrial development in favor of importing munitions and industrial products to achieve a more rapid and immediate military development.

Even as China tried to organize what industry it had for its wartime needs, it had to face three hard facts. Firstly, its own production of munitions depended largely on imported materials. Secondly, its own production could never come close to supplying China's needs in the war, hence the war effort was highly dependent on foreign munitions. Thirdly,

After the fall of Shanghai Japanese soldiers rest in the ruins of shattered buildings

as the Chinese government became territorially established in the more remote and inaccessible parts of China as called for by its defense plan, foreign supplies and materials had an increasingly difficult time reaching its armies and factories. Between July 1937 and November 1938, an estimated 60,000 tons per month reached China through the British port of Hong Kong. Another 2,000 tons per month came in through Hanoi in French Indo-china, connected with Kunming in Yunnan by rail and road. After 1937 Russian supplies reached China from the railhead in Russian Turkestan over the ancient silk caravan route through Sinkiang to northwest China. This route brought more war materials to China than did the Burma Road which opened in 1938. In addition, 60,000 tons of ammunition were shipped to China from the Soviet Black Sea port of Odessa.

In view of their dependence on foreign supplies and the inaccessible nature of their territorial base, one of the basic war policies of the Chinese had to be to secure their lines of communication and supply with the

Above: In 1937-38 the port of Hong Kong was a main entry point for war materials for China. *Below:* Japanese troops advance along a river rather than force a path through dense jungle during the invasion of Burma

Colonel Jack Jouett. He led an American mission to assist the Chinese air force

Captain Claire Chennault. He took service in China in 1937 as an advisor to the Chinese air force

outside world. Realizing early how few and how precarious were their routes of supply, the Chinese were anxious to open another and more secure route. Thus in 1937 and 1938 100,000 coolies hewed by hand an all-weather road from Kunming in Yunnan across the southern spur of the Himalayas to Lashio in northern Burma. Supplies were docked in Rangoon, shipped up the Irrawaddy river to Lashio and thence to China over what came to be known as the Burma Road. As other lines of communication were cut one by one, the preservation of the Burma Road assumed ever greater importance to the Chinese as their one link with the outside world. It is for this reason that Chiang Kai-shek volunteered his best troops, the German-trained and equipped Fifth and Sixth Armies, to assist in the defense of Burma in 1942. The move did not forestall the fall of Burma and the closing of the Burma Road but did cost Chiang his armies which were virtually shattered in the campaign.

In addition to the need to import most of its war material, China was heavily dependent on foreign military assistance to prosecute the war. A thirty-man German military mission had been employed by the Chinese to train and equip their army since 1933 but the mission was recalled after the outbreak of hostilities with Japan. An Italian aviation group was training the Chinese air force in the early 1930s but was gradually supplanted by an American group led by Colonel Jack Jouett. As the air force became more American-oriented, more Americans were drawn to China's service as private citizens, including in 1937 a retired air force captain named Claire Chennault.

After the Japanese attack on Shanghai in August 1937, the Chinese issued an official call for assistance to the major powers. Only the Soviet Union responded – out of its own concern for Japanese intentions toward its eastern borders. By maintaining China in the war against Japan, the Soviet Union could assure itself of its own security in the east and thus be free to concentrate on its European areas. A non-aggression pact between China and the Soviet Union was signed in August 1937, Soviet loans totalling

$300,000,000 were made to China, and 400 planes were provided to the Chinese air force. 500 Soviet military advisors were attached to the Chinese army under the leadership of Vassily Chuikov, later the defender of Stalingrad, and Georgi Zhukov, soon to become the leading Soviet general of the war. Six squadrons of the Soviet air force also fought in China until the outbreak of war in Europe. A road stretching 1,700 miles from Lanchow to the Soviet border was built and Soviet equipment sufficient for the reorganization of fifteen Chinese divisions poured into China between 1938 and 1940. When a Japanese advance into Inner Mongolia threatened this supply line, the Soviets moved in an armored division and a squadron of bombers to protect it. The Japanese stopped short of engaging these forces and withdrew. From 1937 to 1941 the Soviet Union was the major source of foreign assistance to China.

After 1939 when Chiang Kai-shek and the Chinese communists under Mao Tse-tung came to a final parting of the ways, Soviet aid was gradually withdrawn from the central government and a small part redirected to its communist adversaries. The Soviets had profited considerably from their assistance to China. Beyond reducing the ability of Japan to menace Soviet interests in the Far East, the Russians had blooded a large number of pilots in combat, had been able to measure the military capabilities of both the Chinese and Japanese, and had learned much of German equipment and training methods, both of which they studied carefully.

However, as they became increasingly apprehensive of the growing prospect of war in the west, the Soviets needed all their resources for their own defense and were anxiously searching for a more satisfactory solution to the Japanese threat to their borders in the east than that provided by simply maintaining China in the war. There were also various areas of Sino-Soviet friction which

President Franklin Roosevelt. He pledged American aid to China in March 1941

made the Soviets less enthusiastic about assistance to the régime of Chiang Kai-shek. In April 1941, the Russians effected a more satisfactory solution to their problem in the east by signing a non-aggression pact with Japan, at the same time tacitly recognizing the Japanese puppet state of Manchukuo, and in return gaining recognition by Japan of the Mongolian People's Republic. Abandoned by one benefactor, China now became totally dependent on the other major Pacific power with an important stake in the developing Far Eastern war.

Until Pearl Harbor was attacked on 7th December 1941, the United States was merely a sympathetic bystander in the Sino-Japanese conflict. Although America wanted generally to retain China's friendship and preserve her territorial integrity and independence, American policy, both political and military, was neither clearcut nor firmly established. The United States had for some time seen Chinese resistance as an obstacle to Japanese expansion and wished to help China to help itself. In March 1941, President Franklin Roosevelt made the first announcement of concrete American support for China: 'China expresses the magnificent will of millions of

A close advisor to President Roosevelt, Harry Hopkins was one of the first American officials involved in the planning of aid to China

Secretary of State Cordell Hull. He worked with Hopkins

plain people to resist the dismemberment of their nation. China, through Generalissimo Chiang Kai-shek, asks our help. America has said that she shall have our help.' At first loans were made to China, followed by lend-lease aid in May 1941. In that same month, the first military assistance was given to China when an air mission under General H B Clagett spent a month in Chungking at the request of Chiang Kai-shek. The purpose of the mission was to make a report on the Chinese air force to serve as a basis for American aid. A particular concern of the mission was the American Volunteer Group or 'Flying Tigers', a group of private American citizens organized into several fighter squadrons by Claire Chennault with the tacit approval of the American government in August 1941. Despite a lack of equipment and planes, the AVG played a valuable role in the defense of Burma and provided an effective air defense for southwest China.

By the summer of 1941, President Roosevelt, his advisor Harry Hopkins, and Secretary of State Cordell Hull were seriously considering the problems of providing material aid to China in the form of ordnance, motor transport, and military supplies. Lend-lease supplies were moving into China at this time at a rate of 7,500 tons per month over the Burma Road and reached a peak of 12,000 tons in December 1941. The Chinese had requested aid in creating a modern air force, arming thirty divisions, and instituting and maintaining an efficient line of communication into China. Feeling that China did not have the personnel qualified to handle lend-lease aid effectively, Roosevelt established the American Military Mission to China (AMMISCA) in July 1941. The purpose of AMMISCA was to find out precisely what and how much was really needed, how to build on the work of the earlier German military mission, and to render certain organizational and instructional assistance. Led by Brigadier-General John Magruder, the mission was initially composed of six officers experienced in China and prepared to offer expert advice on economic warfare, medicine, railroad management, artillery, and pursuit aircraft. By November the mission had grown to two-thirds of its strength or twenty officers. Thus, at the outbreak of war in December, a foundation had already been laid for Sino-American

General John Magruder led the American military mission to China in July 1941

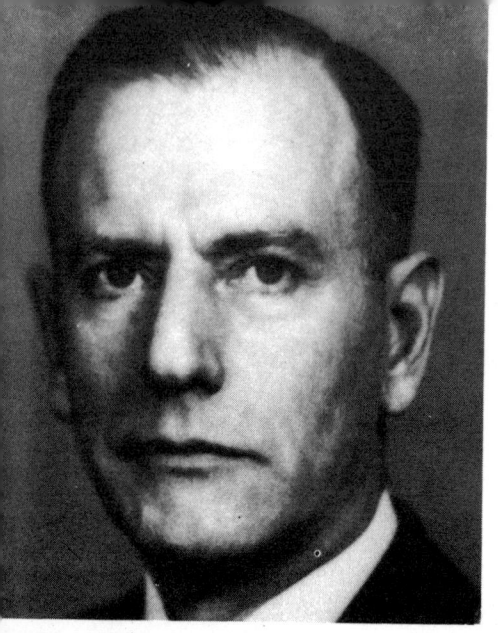

military cooperation.

The entry of the United States into the Far Eastern war and Japan's new commitments in the Pacific should have given China renewed hope, but American observers found her war-weary and her resistance weakening under a pronounced material and moral deterioration. Her own productive powers were so slight and her external communications so poor that a monumental effort was necessary to bolster her war effort. Yet such a monumental effort was not to be made. At the Arcadia Conference of December 1941-January 1942, Roosevelt, Churchill and the Anglo-Ameri-

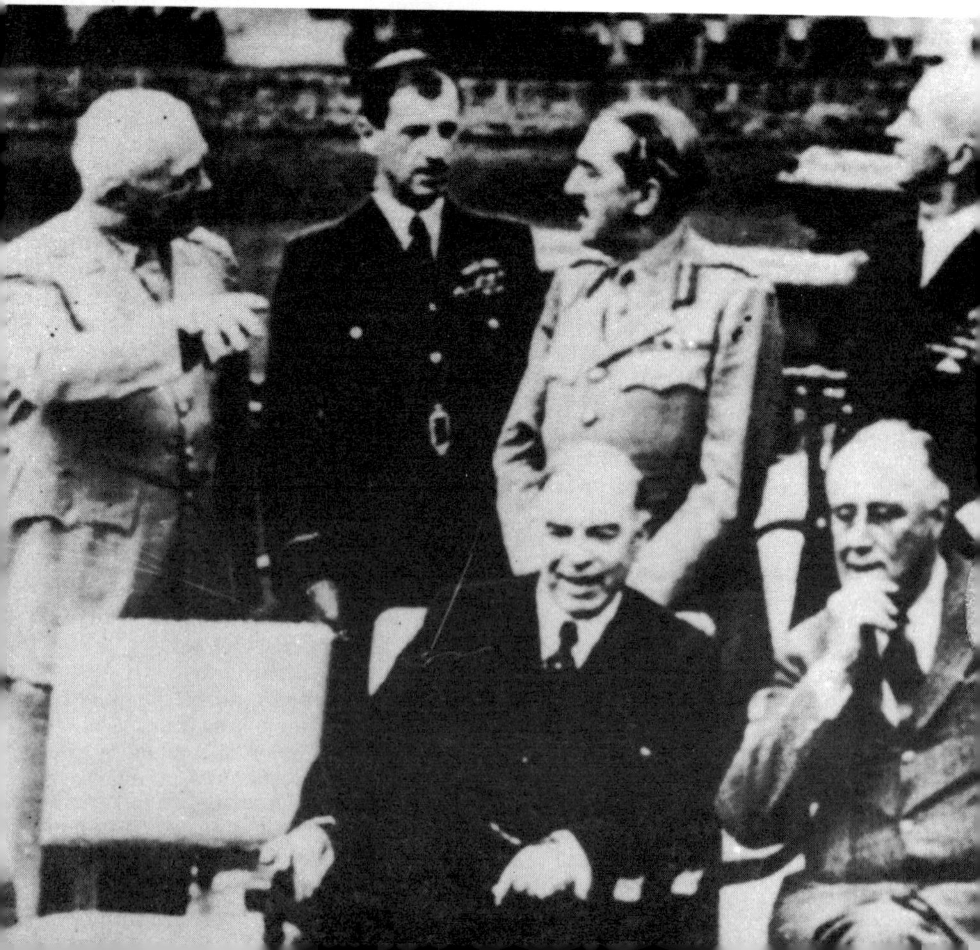

can Combined Chiefs of Staff laid plans for the prosecution of the war which relegated to least importance the China Theater. The strategy developed at this conference and basically adhered to for the duration of the war identified Germany as the chief enemy, hence the Atlantic and Europe were to be the areas of chief effort. Basic aspects of this strategy were defense of the production areas in North America and Britain, maintenance of lines of communications, forging and tightening a ring around Germany, weakening her by indirect methods and a concentrated bomber attack, and eventual invasion. In the Pacific, only those positions would be defended as would 'safeguard vital interests and deny Japan access to needed raw materials'. The startling

Japanese successes in 1942 did not change the overall Allied strategy but did force it to be evaluated in its applications as more forces had to be diverted to the Far East.

Although unable to provide much assistance to China, the United States did want to keep China in the war both for sentimental reasons and immediate military expediency. China contained large Japanese forces which the Allies did not want released for service elsewhere and also constituted a significant and continuous drain on Japanese resources. China also offered the possibility of air bases within

Mackenzie King of Canada, Franklin Roosevelt of the US, and Winston Churchill of Britain at the Arcadia Conference in Quebec

General Joseph Stilwell, Allied Chief of Staff in CBI, reviews Chinese troops training at Ramgarh, India

reach of Japan's vital sea communications and even of the home islands. To give him formal status and placate him, Chiang Kai-shek was appointed Supreme Allied Commander in the China Theater. Lieutenant-General Joseph W Stilwell was made Allied Chief of Staff, deputy commander in China under Chiang, commander of all American forces in the China-Burma-India Theater, and supervisor of lend-lease aid. His directive was generally described as 'increasing the effectiveness of the United States' assistance to the Chinese government for the prosecution of the war and assisting in improving the combat efficiency of the Chinese army.' From the beginning, Stilwell was doomed to failure by the multiplicity and competing nature of his duties, lack of resources and support, and the impossibility of a theater of war stretching 2,000 miles from Karachi to Sian.

The Japanese were in turn having their own problems. Instead of the quick victory on which they had planned, the war dragged on in a stalemate and required a heavy commitment of their resources. According to Japanese sources, twenty-seven of her fifty-one divisions were tied down

A Japanese supply column in French Indo-China after the Vichy administration capitulated to Japanese demands

in China in 1941. Unable to force a decision on the battlefield or to bring the intractable Chiang Kai-shek to the negotiating table for a political settlement, Japan adopted a war strategy emphasizing the blockade of China. The Japanese were well aware that Chiang's government was cut off from its former sources of income and support, dependent on the undeveloped resources of western China and foreign assistance, and faced with a steadily deteriorating internal situation. General Sugiyama put this policy into effect in 1941, hoping to strangle China by cutting off all of her external sources of supplies and support.

Already in control of China's coastal areas, it remained for the Japanese to cut off the three remaining supply routes to China. The Soviet-Japanese non-aggression pact of April 1941 brought a final halt to Russian support of China and also freed 100,000 troops of Japan's crack Kwantung Army for use elsewhere. At the same time,

Japanese attention was focused on French Indo-china which was seen not only as a supply route for China but a source of rice, rubber, and coal for Japan and a springboard for possible operations to the south. After a series of negotiations, ultimatums and a brief but bloody clash between French and Japanese troops, the Vichy administration in Indo-China capitulated, leaving Japan in complete control of the French colony in July 1941. The Hanoi-Kunming route thus came to an end.

The Burma Road was now China's last line of communication. Knowing full well that Britain was fighting a life and death battle on its home front, Japan had been applying pressure to have the road closed. In July 1940 Churchill had agreed to close the road but reopened it three months later. Prior to 1941, no particular importance had been placed on Burma as a military objective but with the German destruction of British and French power in Europe and the pro-Axis faction now firmly in control in Tokyo, new adventures were planned in South-East Asia. Burma became an attractive target because its occupation would cut China's last line of communication and enable the Japanese to strike at the hitherto inaccessible rear areas in south-west China. Prospects were good for knocking China out of the war once and for all. In late December 1941, a powerful Japanese invasion was launched by 100,000 troops supported by 700 planes. British and Chinese opposition was swept aside and Lashio taken in April 1942. Japanese forces then drove up the Burma Road toward the Yunnan border and were halted only at the Salween river gorge by a last desperate stand of Chinese troops supported by intensive air strikes by the American Volunteer Group which prevented the Japanese from crossing the river. Elsewhere British forces were driven completely out of Burma except for a small outpost called Fort Hertz in the northernmost area.

General Henry Arnold told Roosevelt that an India-China air route was essential. *Below:* Jubilant Japanese troops in Rangoon cheer the fall of the city

China was now truly isolated and in grave danger of succumbing to Japanese pressure and its own internal weaknesses. Concerned about China's declining ability to resist, Roosevelt again pledged American support: 'The Japanese may have cut the Burma Road but I want to say to the gallant people of China that no matter what advances the Japanese may make, ways will be found to deliver airplanes and munitions to the armies of China. We remember that the Chinese people were the first to stand up and fight against the aggressors in this war.' As early as February 1942, the commander of the Army Air Force (AAF), Henry Arnold, told Roosevelt that an air route from India to China must be developed in view of the probable loss of Rangoon. Roosevelt was enthusiastic and immediately informed Chiang Kai-shek that an air route would be maintained even if the land route remained open. He hoped that this would allay both Chiang's discontent over the small secondary support to be given to China and Chiang's fear that China would be totally cut off.

The isolation of China and the subsequent need to rely solely on air supply meant that all hope of using China as a main theater of ground warfare had to be abandoned. Chinese forces could not be built up to fight an offensive war but would have to maintain their defensive war from the mountainous interior. While the outcome of the war was being determined in other theaters, the air route over the 'hump' would serve to bring a trickle of supplies and a ray of hope to the embattled Chinese and hopefully keep them occupying large numbers of Japanese troops which might otherwise be used against the Allies elsewhere.

The hump begins

Tenth Air Force C-47s on their way to
drop parapack supplies to advanced CBI
outposts

The Japanese onslaught launched in December 1941 largely destroyed the Allied defense plans in Asia as the Philippines, Netherlands East Indies, Malaya, and Burma all fell in the first half of 1942. Allied forces were in full retreat to Australia and India. A Japanese invasion of India loomed as a serious possibility in view of air attacks on eastern India and the strong enemy naval presence in the Bay of Bengal. Most of America's Pacific air power had been destroyed in the first wave of Japanese attacks. Of 600 planes based in the Pacific area, less than 200 had survived. While China's position was seen as vital to the war effort in theory, the China-Burma-India Theater (CBI) in practice enjoyed the lowest priority of all theaters of war in the allocation of resources, a fact which meant that CBI remained starved for men and material throughout the war. Despite Roosevelt's firmly expressed statement early in 1942 that 'it is obviously of the utmost urgency that the pathway to China be kept open', the development of the air route to China was to come neither quickly nor easily in the first confused year of world wide war.

CBI was primarily a British and Chinese theater. For the United States, it was almost entirely an air rather than a ground theater. There were never more than a few thousand American tactical ground troops in CBI, mainly OSS and commando units such as Merrill's Marauders. Stilwell arrived in February 1942 to serve as theater commander. Major-General Louis Brereton arrived the following month to take command of the main American unit in the theater, the Tenth Air Force, which had been activated on 12th February 1942 at Patterson Field, Ohio. The creation of the Tenth Air Force was a logical step in American policy since the main American commitment in CBI was maintaining China in the war through air supply.

Arriving in India from the Nether-

lands East Indies where he had commanded the American air units until the fall of the Dutch colony, Brereton brought with him eight heavy bombers, their crews, and a few staff officers. Within a few weeks, these were augmented by ten P-40 fighters sent from Australia. He did not command the American Volunteer Group, the only other American unit in the theater, which was not inducted into the air force as the 23rd Fighter Group until July. Brereton's headquarters squadron, the ground echelons of his tactical groups, and the personnel and planes of his one transport group did not reach India until mid-May. Initially, Brereton had literally nothing with which to fight or to launch the air route to China. Such were the modest beginnings of the Tenth Air Force.

The problems requiring priority action were the air route to China, the organization of an Operations Training Unit to complete the tactical training of newly arriving squadrons, and construction of airdromes usable by heavy bombers and transports. The air route rated top priority. Brereton's chief of staff, Brigadier-General Earl Naiden, was personally charged with command control of the entire operation and separated from any other staff duty by the War Department in Washington. Highly unacceptable to Brereton, this act raised the first of a long series of conflicts about command responsibilities, conflicts which were to characterize CBI throughout the war. Brereton argued that routes flown and airdromes used were common to both transport and tactical units, that the Tenth Air Force was responsible for general security, and that the theater air commander must have the right to employ all aircraft in support of tactical operations when necessary. General Robert Olds of the Air Corps Ferrying Command replied that such an arrangement would result in diversions from transport to combat operations. The War Department decided that Stilwell was to

Above: An American SBD dive-bomber destroyed by Japanese planes at Henderson Field, the Philippines, December 1941. *Below:* The fall of Malaya; Japanese soldiers run toward the railroad station in Kwala Lumpur as government buildings burn in the background

General Louis Brereton, the first commander of the Tenth Air Force in CBI

General Earl Naiden, responsible for the initial planning of the air route to China

control the Assam-China route, Brereton the trans-India route, and the War Department itself policies concerning movement and supply. This was a confusing solution but did permit centralized control of strategic air services while not entirely ignoring the prerogatives of theater command.

The dispute over control of the India-China transport operations in CBI reflected a larger conflict then going on in the AAF. In 1941 a ferrying command had been created within the air force specifically to handle the strategic movement of high priority personnel, supplies, and planes on a global basis. The system was not working well in 1942 as theater commanders made a practice of commandeering personnel and supplies en route to other theaters. The argument was that a commander had control of all troops and material in his theater even if these were in transit. The Ferrying Command countered that this was robbing Peter to pay Paul and that it was unable to carry out its functions as a result. In July 1942 the Air Ferrying Command was renamed the Air Transport Command (ATC)

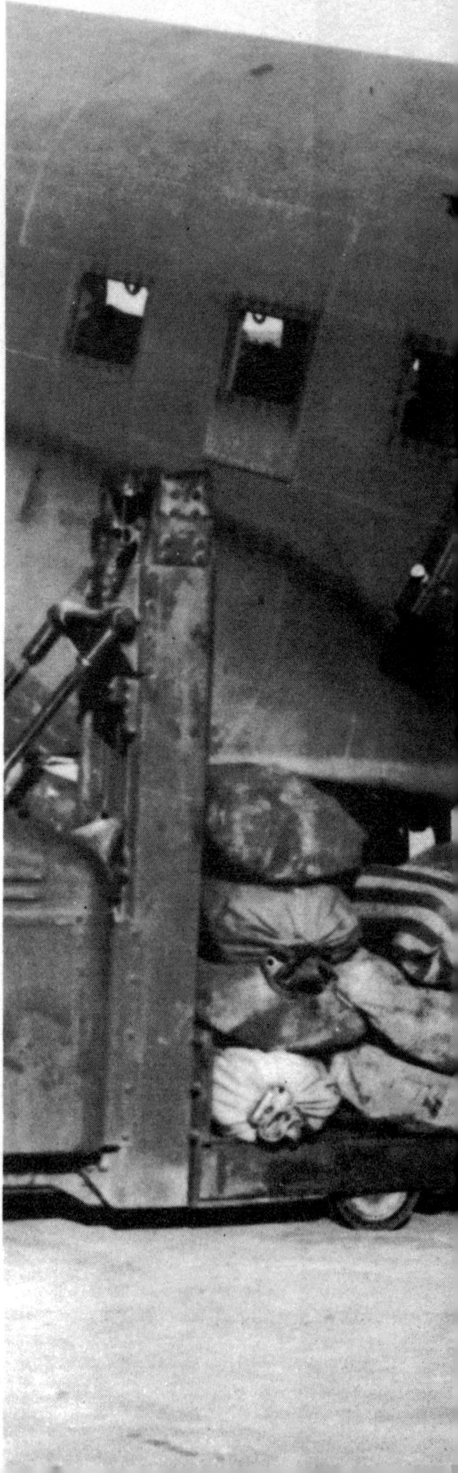

Above: General Harold George, the first commander of the Air Transport Command. *Right:* Mail sacks are loaded onto an ATC C-47 in Karachi, India

under General Harold George with C R Smith, President of American Airlines, as his deputy. The concept of ATC as a centralised strategic transport service directed from the War Department in Washington was accepted shortly thereafter, enabling ATC to pursue its mission in close cooperation with but independent of the various theater commands. In two years, ATC was to grow from a few officers and clerks to 85,000 officers and men operating half a dozen major airways with branch and feeder lines throughout the world. The ATC-theater command issue was shortly to return to CBI.

Initial plans for the air route were to build up the China National Aviation Corporation (CNAC) to twenty-five aircraft to maintain 'essential communications' between Calcutta and Kunming. CNAC was a Sino-American venture owned forty-five per cent by Pan-American Airlines and fifty-five per cent by the Chinese government. It was a well organized, efficient operation which clearly dem-

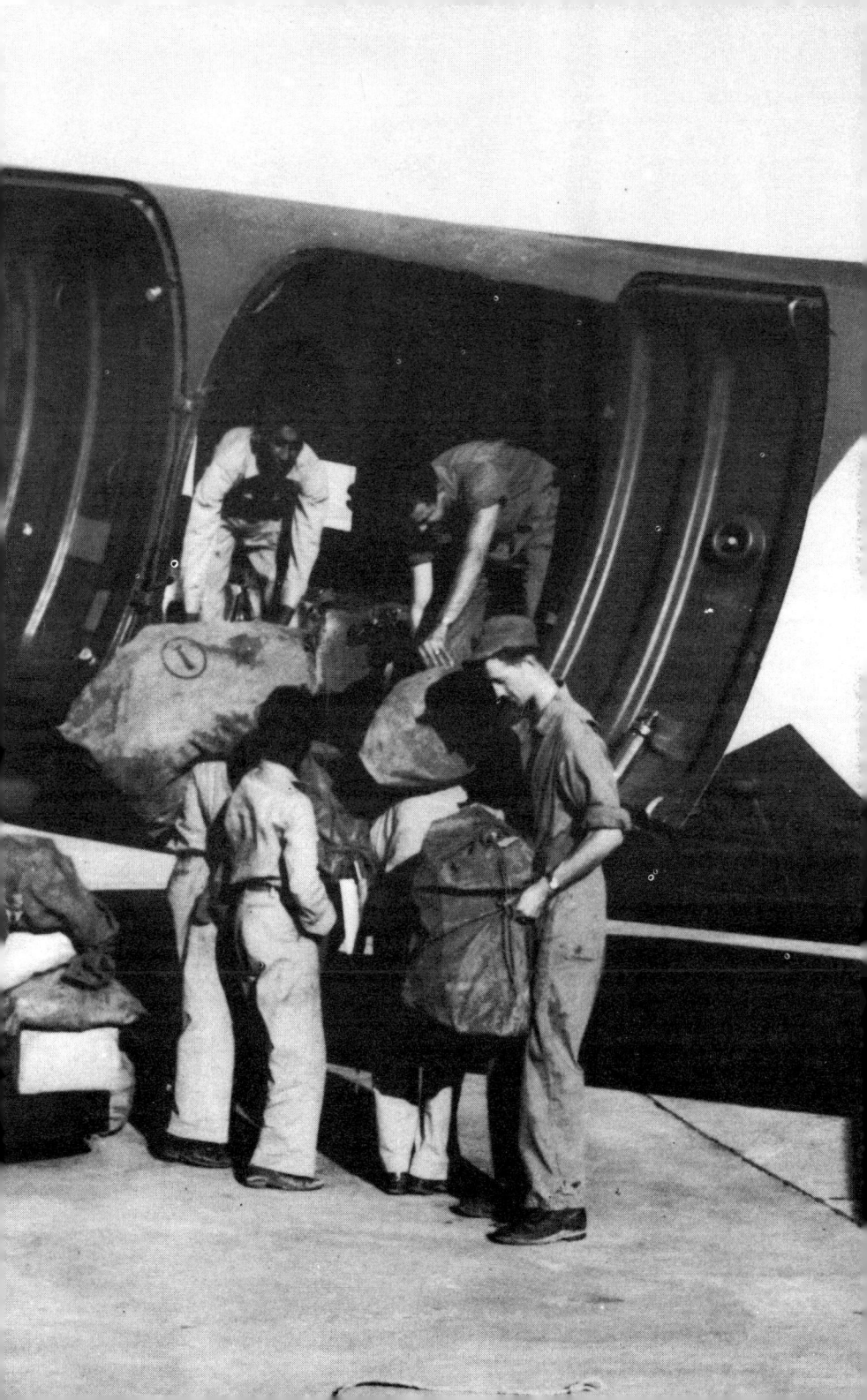

Lost to the Japanese in 1942 and recaptured in 1944, the Myitkyina airbase in north Burma was vital to the airlift

onstrated the difference between experienced airline management and the inexperience of the AAF in transport operations. In September 1943, CNAC planes carried forty-nine tons of cargo per plane compared with twenty-three tons for ATC planes. At the end of 1944, CNAC planes had made 35,000 trips between India and China. In 1944 CNAC delivered 41,000 tons of cargo to China compared with 230,000 tons by ATC with its vastly greater resources. But the War Department was reluctant to depend on an organization which it did not control, so it determined to establish its own air transport route to China. Ten planes were, however, turned over to CNAC to enlarge its operations. Thus CNAC and ATC were destined to fly side by side but independently of each other.

Foreseeing the loss of Rangoon, the War Department ordered Brereton shortly after his arrival to survey air routes to Chungking. The task of planning the transport service to China was given to his chief of staff, General Naiden. It was believed that upper and central Burma would be successfully defended against the advancing Japanese, so the supply route could run from Assam through upper Burma to China. Naiden's proposal was to fly cargo from the Royal Air Force (RAF) base at Dinjan in Assam to Myitkyina in upper Burma, a distance of 200 air miles over the Naga Hills. Cargo would then be sent by barge 100 miles down the Irrawaddy river to Bhamo and thence to China over the Burma Road. The only airdrome in Assam suitable for transports was the RAF field at Dinjan whereas at least three fields were needed. The approaching monsoon in Assam meant that no more fields could be made ready before the fall. The airdrome at Myitkyina could be put in shape by May but again the monsoon would prevent the preparation of other fields until the fall. Given these facts, Naiden believed that more than twenty-five planes could not be operated and that service would be uncertain because of the weather during the monsoon.

Due to Japanese air attacks on eastern India, supplies had to be shipped in through the west Indian port of Karachi. Given the nature of the Indian transportation system, it quickly became apparent that an air service between Karachi and Dinjan was needed as much as between Assam and China. Within the Tenth Air Force, Brereton therefore established the Trans-India Ferry Command to move cargo from Karachi to Assam and the Assam-Burma-China Ferry Command to handle the Burma-China route. In theory the two commands were separate but the distinction was not clear in practice because neither manpower nor space at Dinjan was sufficient to permit the trans-shipment of all cargo. Trans-India planes were often simply refueled and sent on to Burma or China.

The ABC Ferry Command established itself at Dinjan with ten DC-3s borrowed from the trans-Africa route operated by Pan American Airlines and three AAF C-47s. Dinjan was also the base of two RAF squadrons and was so crowded that it was impossible to disperse properly parked aircraft. There were only a few RAF fighters available for defense against air attack, no anti-aircraft batteries, and no air warning system. Consequently the Americans got all their planes into the air at dawn with any service or cargo operations necessary in daylight handled as expeditiously as possible. Since barracks were still under construction, the men lived in mud and bamboo *bashas* with dirt floors. Quartered ten miles from the airdrome, the Americans were entirely dependent on the British for ground transportation since they had none of their own. Messing facilities were poor and the food worse.

The first task assigned to the ABC Ferry Command was to haul 30,000 gallons of aviation gasoline and 500 gallons of lubricants to China for the

General 'Jimmy' Doolittle wires a Japanese medal to a 500-lb bomb to be used by his Tokyo raiders in April 1942

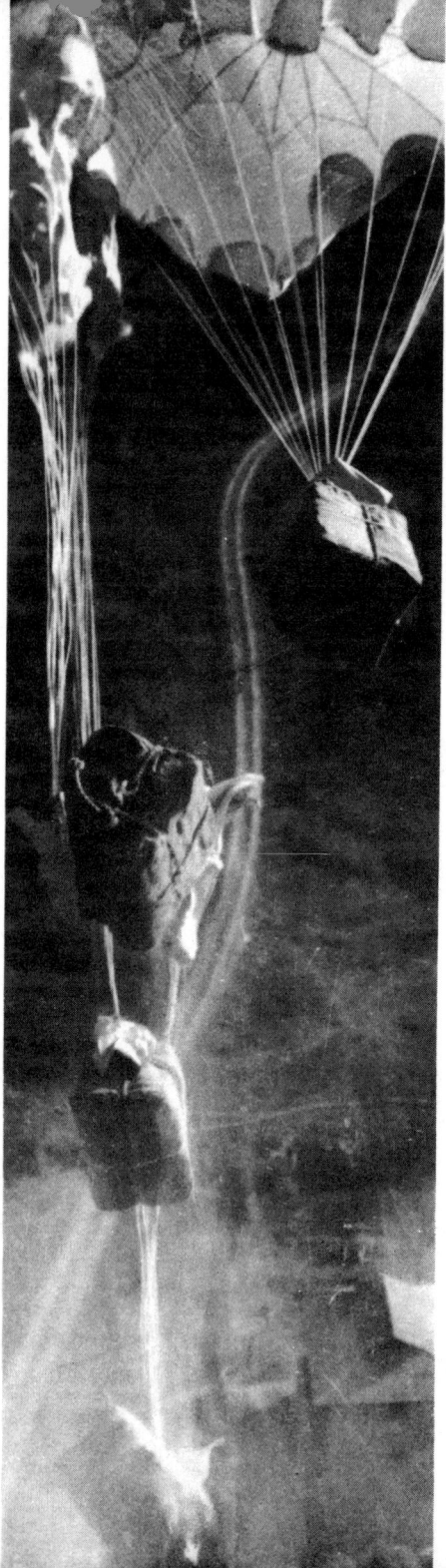

A supply drop from a Tenth Air Force C-47 over Burma. These drops saved thousands of troops and refugees in 1942

use of the Doolittle Tokyo raiders after their mission. As it turned out, Doolittle's planes never needed the supplies as all crashed in China. Doolittle himself was later flown out over the hump on an ABC Ferry Command run.

The next task was emergency deliveries of ammunition, fuel, and supplies to Allied forces in Burma, with loads of wounded troops and civilians on the return runs. Although crews were badly overworked and at the mercy of enemy fighters, not a plane was lost. As Allied defenses crumbled, the emphasis on supply was changed to evacuation. Between April and June, the Tenth Air Force evacuated 4,499 passengers and 900 tons of cargo, the RAF evacuated 4,117 persons, and CNAC pilots reportedly flew out close to 10,000 people. Flying C-47s built to carry twenty-four passengers and fly at a maximum altitude of 12,000 feet, American and British pilots routinely flew fifty or more passengers at altitudes of 18,000 feet over the hump. As the retreat turned into a rout, supplies had to be dropped to the columns of troops and refugees trekking out of Burma to India. A special problem were the Chinese armies scattered over upper Burma struggling back to Yunnan with heavy losses from starvation and cholera. ABC Ferry Command pilots dropped 2,000 tons of rice, salt, and medicine to these troops. Most of Stilwell's staff were evacuated by air but the general himself refused air evacuation and spent five weeks walking out of Burma to Assam, an act which was militarily inexcusable for a theater commander but which earned him fame in the American press.

When the Japanese climaxed their drive in Burma by taking Myitkyina on 8th May, Allied ground resistance came to an end with two consequences

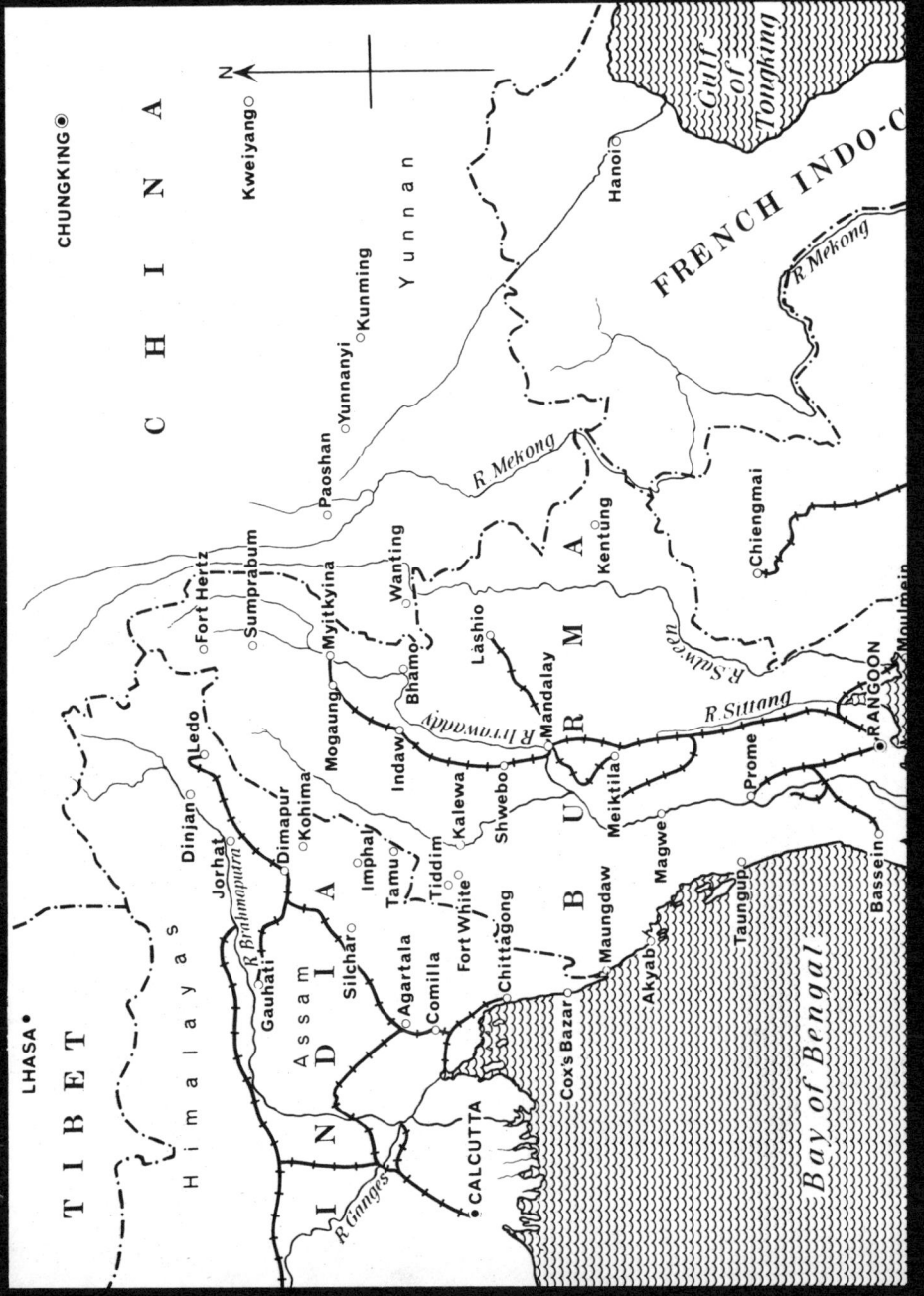

Area of hump operations

for the Tenth Air Force. Originally the key base in the air route to China, Myitkyina now became a serious threat to the air route because it lay within easy striking distance of the Allied base at Dinjan for enemy fighters and bombers. Brereton countered this threat with a series of heavy bomber attacks on Myitkyina which rendered it unusable for a time. On a broader scale, the Japanese conquest of Burma raised questions about the mission of the Tenth Air Force. Should it be limited to the defense of India until the security of

The northern or true hump route entailed flying through worse weather and over higher mountains than the southerly route originally planned

India had been assured against the Japanese forces in Burma and the Bay of Bengal? Had the early conceptions of an air transport route to China been overly optimistic? The supply line had turned out to be longer than anticipated while the loss of Myitkyina as a base meant that a more northerly route from Assam to Yunnan would have to be used, a route which necessitated flying over much higher mountains and through worse weather, the true hump route. This in turn meant new operational hazards and heavier demands on equipment and personnel. But as the Japanese naval threat in the Indian Ocean receded, it became obvious that not Ceylon but Port Moresby in New Guinea was the next enemy objective.

So as the mission of the Tenth emerged unchanged, its energies were again focused on building up its forces and establishing the new transport route over the hump.

While the Tenth Air Force was struggling to establish itself in India, preparations were underway in the United States to launch the hump operations. At the first meeting of the Anglo-American Combined Chiefs of Staff in December 1941, it was already recognized that supplies would most likely have to reach China by air, so transports would have to be sent to CBI at once. The American Joint Chiefs of Staff, meeting in January 1942, then began to consider how to create adequate transport capabilities in CBI, a problem mainly the responsibility of Henry Arnold, Commander of the AAF. The basic question was where to get the planes and crews to be sent to CBI.

In the spring of 1942, the AAF had only 216 transports for the entire war effort. First priority went to the airborne components of the projected cross-channel assault in Europe (Operation BOLERO), second priority to the Air Ferry Command for its operations, and third priority to the China airlift. BOLERO was assigned 139 transports, the Air Ferry Command fifty seven, and the airlift none. At that time it was a common but erroneous estimate in Washington that seventy-five planes could fly 5,000 tons per month to China from India: 3,500 lend-lease and 1,500 for Chennault. With no

The Douglas DC-3 Dakota. The most widely used transport aircraft of the Second
 World War, if not of all time, the DC-3 was produced initially before the war as a
civil airliner. Its merits were seen immediately, and it was produced in large numbers
(over 10,000) during the war years for use with the Allies. The basic design was very
rugged, and could therefore be used in the troop transport role with little
modification. But for the transport of war material it was produced in a special
military version, the C-47, which had a strengthened fuselage floor and larger
loading doors on the port side. *Speed:* 230mph maximum, 167mph cruising.
Range: 1,300 miles. *Crew:* 3. *Load:* 9,028lbs of cargo or up to 24 fully-equipped
troops

The Douglas C-47 Skytrain. Derived from the civil DC-3 Dakota airliner, the C-47 was the basic medium transport aircraft in service with the US air forces in South-East Asia at the beginning of the war. The main differences between the civil and military versions was the strengthening of the fuselage floor and the undercarriage, together with the fitting of larger doors in the fuselage for the loading of military cargo, which can include (in one load) two jeeps or three aircraft engines, or a similar weight in other stores, or alternatively 28 fully-armed men. *Engines:* Two Pratt & Whitney R-1930 Twin Wasp radials, 1,050hp each. *Armament:* None. *Speed:* 230mph at 8,500 feet. *Climb:* 1,130 feet per minute. *Ceiling:* 23,200 feet. *Range:* 2,125 miles. *Weight empty/loaded:* 16,865/30,000 lbs. *Span:* 95 feet. *Length:* 64 feet 6 inches

Chinese Ambassador T V Soong applied heavy pressure to Roosevelt to get the airlift moving

experience of these pilots ranged from 1,800 to 10,000 hours of flying time in multi-engined transport craft, but briefing was necessary on long range over-water flight. In late April and early May, a steady stream of planes and crews left Florida for India via the Brazil-West Africa-Middle East route.

Again under pressure from the Chinese representative in Washington, T V Soong, Roosevelt sent Arnold a memo on 5th May expressing concern about the air route. Arnold replied that he planned to have seventy-five C-47s on the China run as soon as planes and crews could be found, a reply which satisfied both Roosevelt and Soong at the time. By June ten C-53s had been delivered as promised to CNAC and thirty-nine C-47s to the Tenth Air Force.

Just when it appeared that the hump operations might seriously get started, the course of the war elsewhere caused the Tenth Air Force to be stripped of fifty per cent of its operational strength. Early in 1942, all air units in CBI were placed on call for duty in the Middle East should the situation so require. In June British forces were being pressed back against the Suez Canal after the fall of Tobruk. Brereton was ordered to the Middle East to assist the British with all available bombers, all personnel necessary for his Middle East headquarters, and all necessary transport planes. He was also given authority to appropriate India-bound cargo and equipment passing through the Middle East. A squadron of light bombers en route to China was diverted to his command. In addition, lend-lease supplies stockpiled in India for China were diverted to the Middle East and the Soviet Union, at that time reeling under a powerful German invasion. Naiden was left to carry on as best he could with a skeleton staff, a crippled air transport system, and virtually no combat strength other than Chennault's modest forces in China. The hump lift was severely retarded by

transports on hand and under heavy Chinese diplomatic pressure to reach 3,500 tons of lend-lease per month, Arnold in desperation proposed converting fifty B-24 bombers into transports for the airlift. The Operations Planning Division in the War Department opposed this move strongly because it felt that the bombers were needed for BOLERO and that the airlift was only a token operation. Stilwell sent repeated messages warning Washington not to build up Chinese hopes because only five to ten per cent of the lend-lease allotment then being discussed could possibly be airlifted. So meager were the resources of the AAF at this point that in February Arnold was finally ordered by Roosevelt to commandeer twenty-five DC-3s from the civilian airlines to start the airlift.

In March, over 100 airline pilots holding reserve commissions in the AAF were called to active duty to provide the crews for the airlift. From these came the nucleus of the 1st Ferrying Group which assembled at Morrison Field, Florida. No extensive training was necessary since the

Above: The C-53 was little used by ATC but saw some service on CNAC runs over the hump. *Below:* The C-47 was the workhorse of the hump until replaced by the C-46. Here ATC C-47s fly in formation over China

this turn of events. May saw eighty tons delivered, 106 in June, and seventy-three in July. No significant progress was made until December when tonnage jumped to 1,226.

The summer of 1942 was the first of many crises in Sino-American relations during the war. American commitments and promises to China could not be kept because of the military situation in other theaters. On learning of Brereton's orders, Stilwell wrote in his diary: 'Now what can I say to the G-mo? We fail in *all* our commitments, and blithely tell him to just carry on, old top.' Already fretting over his failure to receive the help he thought was owed to China, Chiang Kai-shek ordered Stilwell to get a yes or no answer on whether or not the Allies considered the China Theater necessary and would support it. After an initially non-commital reply by Roosevelt, Chiang demanded three American divisions to help the Chinese reopen a land route to China, 500 planes for the Tenth Air Force, and 5,000 tons a month over the hump. Roosevelt finally answered that by early 1943 there would be 500 planes for the Tenth and 100 transports for the hump; there would also be lend-lease to equip the Chinese divisions then in India, and as much lend-lease as could be flown over the hump. Chiang accepted this statement but episodes similar to the 'Three Demands Crisis' were to occur later. For the first time, American policy makers began to realize how critical was the situation with Chiang and how loose the Sino-American ties were becoming as a result of American inability to meet the commitments made to China.

The dismal lack of progress with the hump operations through the summer of 1942 led to another proposal to turn the route over to the highly successful CNAC. Stilwell quickly vetoed the idea on the grounds that he did not want military personnel under civilian control in a combat area and that he doubted CNAC would haul only war

General Clayton Bissell succeeded Brereton as commander of the Tenth Air Force

material. He instead proposed leasing planes from CNAC to build up the hump route, to which Chiang Kai-shek agreed. Since Brereton's forces in the Middle East were unlikely to return to CBI for an indefinite period, Stilwell requested the War Department to relieve these of their assignment to the Tenth Air Force and to provide replacements. As Naiden was to be sent to the United States for hospitalization, Stilwell requested that his air advisor, Brigadier-General Clayton Bissell, be named commander of the Tenth in August.

The failure of the air route to China had been largely responsible for Bissell's appointment and he was constantly reminded that this was his most urgent mission. One of his first acts was to reorganize the Tenth Air Force into the India Air Task Force under Brigadier-General Caleb Haynes, the China Air Task Force under Chennault, the India-China Ferry Command under Colonel Robert Tate, the Tenth Air Service Command under Colonel Robert Oliver, and the Karachi American Air Base Command under Brigadier-General Francis Brady.

Bissell faced numerous problems in trying to develop the hump. Morale among his troops was very low due to a lack of newspapers, books, feminine companionship, and tobacco. The troops had not been paid or received mail for months and suffered from the heat, humidity, dust, bad food, and poor housing. There was a critical shortage of equipment in all categories. Replacement troops and new units often arrived without their equipment which appeared much later if at all. The pilfering of supplies en route by other commands resulted in acute shortages in CBI. Due to the poor record of the Tenth to date, Bissell was under constant fire from General Arnold about the shortcomings of his command in various areas. A strong mutual dislike also existed between Bissell and Chennault, over whom Bissell had been given one day's seniority in promotion, dating back to their days together at the Air Force Tactical School in 1931. Clearly Bissell was not to have an easy time of it.

In spite of all these problems plus the monsoon, the loss of the Burma bases, and the loss of planes to the Middle East, the hump tonnage began to improve. After the low period of the summer when deliveries fell below those of the previous spring, Bissell had every available plane flying the hump. The highest priority was given to aircraft maintenance, an absolute necessity to keep planes in service. Airdrome construction was rushed by transferring service troops to Assam. The September tonnage showed an appreciable increase as a result of Bissell's efforts. By October, airdrome construction had progressed far enough for Bissell to announce that he could operate seventy-five transports if these were available. The October lift showed another increase but before Bissell's efforts could really bear fruit, Stilwell was notified that as of 1st December, the Air Transport Command was to take charge of the India-China route.

Until the end of 1942, the air route to China moved an insignificant amount of supplies. Had Chennault's China Air Task Force not been the recipient of gasoline, bombs, and ammunition hoarded by the Chinese while the Burma Road was open, it would have gone out of business in the summer and at one point in the winter of 1943 was in fact grounded for a month for lack of gasoline. The reasons for the failure of the hump lift were varied. Of the sixty-two C-47s delivered by December 1942, fifteen had been destroyed, four were still with Brereton in the Middle East, and the remaining forty-three were often out of commission for lack of spare engines and parts. These planes not only had to serve the hump run but maintain the trans-India route and were often diverted to meet combat emergencies such as the Burma retreat. Communications were rudimentary – the most powerful radio sets in China had a range of only thirty to fifty miles to give direction to the Bendix Left-Right Indicator. There was no weather reporting to speak of at either Dinjan or Kunming. As one pilot said: 'The present system is if you can see the the end of the runway, it's safe to take off.' Neither pilots nor operations personnel had mastered the techniques required to handle overloads under the weather and altitude conditions of the hump. Ground operations were still primitive. At the end of 1942, planes were still refueled by native laborers pumping gasoline by hand from drums.

The most serious problem, however, appears to have been the mental attitude of Stilwell and Bissell. Since the hump operations were of crucial significance to Chinese defense planning, the Aviation Technical Advisor of China Defense Supplies Inc, Frank Sinclair, made a study of the problem in the fall of 1942. His report flatly characterized Stilwell and Bissell as

Chinese laborers refuel one of the light planes of Chennault's Fourteenth Air Force

'defeatist' in their attitude toward the hump. The commander of the China Air Task Force, Claire Chennault, also felt strongly that the failure of the hump was due not only to the technical problems of air supply but also to the 'contempt' of Stilwell and Bissell for this method of supply. Stilwell was an old-line infantry officer and his ignorance of the potential of air supply was understandable to Chennault but Bissell was a career air force officer and pilot. For him to persist in labeling the hump 'impractical' was inexplicable and incompetent to Chennault who later bitterly accused Stilwell and Bissell of allowing the potential of the hump to go undeveloped until May 1943 when Roosevelt issued a presidential directive on the matter. There is sufficient evidence to indicate that the conclusion of Sinclair and Chennault about the attitude of Stilwell and Bissell was probably justified but it should also be noted that Chennault's was not an unprejudiced viewpoint. His China Air Task Force was totally dependent on the hump lift while he himself was in constant and often heated conflict with both Stilwell and Bissell on a variety of issues.

Sinclair's report on the hump led to the decision to place the India-China transport operation under the control of ATC in December. With full command of all planes, maintenance facilities, spare parts, and personnel connected with the operation, ATC was responsible to General Arnold in Washington, but was to 'work in close harmony with the theater commander but not under his control as far as the conduct of the operation is concerned.' The reasoning was that ATC was devoted to air transport alone while the theater commander was concerned with combat and the preparation for combat. The explanation accepted for the failure of the hump was that the 1st Ferrying Group had been handicapped in its primary mission by diversion to other tasks deemed more urgent by the theater command. Now reconstituted as the India-China Wing of ATC, it would have singleness of purpose and control by an organization solely concerned with air transport. The only mission of the new India-China Wing was 'to get supplies to China and bring back return loads of strategic materials'. Stilwell's air advisor, Colonel Edward Alexander, was named commanding officer of the wing. Brereton had fore-stalled the early effort of the War Department to separate the China transport route from CBI theater operations but only seven months later the issue had been finally and decisively resolved in favor of centralized control and separation.

When ATC took control of the China route, the original plan to provide seventy-five B-24 s was still unfulfilled. ATC therefore prepared to send twelve C-87s and fifty C-46s as soon as possible. This was, however, still far from meeting the commitments made by Roosevelt to Chiang Kai-shek. At the end of 1942, the hump lift was still almost a year away from the beginning of its later brilliant success. China's only link with its Allies remained tenuous.

A C-87 approaches Tezpur airdrome in Assam at the end of a run over the hump

Known as the 'Flying Coffin', the C-46 initally had severe operational and engineering problems

Failure

The Tenth Air Force was responsible for developing the hump lift from March to December 1942, at which time the Air Transport Command was given control by the War Department. In launching the air lift, the Tenth was confronted with a number of problems, most of which were not satisfactorily resolved until almost the end of the war. In one way or another, the Tenth had to contend with the geography and weather over the hump, a severe shortage of aircraft, a difficult maintenance situation, a lack of bases, logistics and supply in the unstable Indian political situation, rescue and survival operations for downed crews, and lastly, attacks by the enemy on the hump route and its terminals in India and China. In the aggregate, these problems were overwhelming for the Tenth as its record over the hump clearly shows. Having the hump as its only concern, the India-China Wing of ATC was better prepared to deal with the situation but, even so, its progress was

ATC planes had to contend with some of the highest mountains and worst weather in the world over the hump

still modest until the summer of 1943.

Assam was chosen as the base area in India for the air route because it is contiguous to both China and Burma. The only airdrome in Assam suitable for transports in early 1942 was Dinjan, lying ninety feet above sea level in the steamy Brahmaputra river valley, 200 air miles from Myitkyina and 500 air miles from Kunming. The typical hump run lasted only a few hours. With its crew of a pilot, co-pilot, engineer, and radioman, a C-47 transport took off from Dinjan flying east out of the Brahmaputra valley. Encountered first was the 10,000-foot Patkai Range, followed by the upper Chindwin river valley and the 14,000-foot Kumon Mountains. A series of 14,000-16,000-foot ridges separated by the valleys of the West Irrawaddy, East Irrawaddy, Salween, and Mekong rivers were a prelude to the 15,000-20,000-foot Santung Range, the main 'hump' which gave its name to the air route. East of the Mekong, the terrain became less rugged and the elevations more moderate on the approach to Kunming. The Dinjan-Myitkyina run used a more southerly route which was not only shorter but enabled transports to fly over mountains about 10,000-feet in elevation. After the Japanese occupation of Burma, the need to use the northern route over the high hump exclusively was a severe setback for the airlift.

The air route passed through the turbulent meeting place of three major Eurasian air masses, hence the hump was famous for its stormy weather. Low pressure masses moving from the west along the main ranges of the Himalayas, highs from the Bay of Bengal, and Siberian lows all clashed in furious conflict at the hump. Violent turbulence, cross winds of 100-150mph, and severe icing were common features of weather over the hump. C-47s were on occasion flipped upside down by turbulence. Flying at 16,000 feet, others were rocketed upward to 28,000 feet by sudden updrafts, then plummeted to 6,000 feet

within two minutes by down drafts. In some cases the descent was so rapid and the leveling off so sudden that cargo ripped out the belly of the plane until special counter measures were taken in rigging cargo. Planes sometimes iced so much that they dropped thousands of feet before vibration and higher temperatures shook off the ice. Others staggered over the hump at 95mph and landed with wings bent and warped from the weight of the ice. In order to avoid icing and turbulence, planes had to fly at 20,000 feet and up. Colonel Edward Alexander, Commander of the India-China Wing, noted in a report: 'The weather here has been pretty awful. The icing level starts at 12,000 feet. Today a C-87 went to 29,500 feet on instruments and was unable to climb any higher, and could not get on top of the overcast.' Pilots sometimes had to make instrument flights all the way from Dinjan to Kunming and return twice a day, seeing the ground only at departure and destination.

The weather over the hump had one point in its favor. It provided unarmed transports with some protection from prowling Japanese fighters and saved many a plane. One pilot flew his C-47 out of a cloud bank and found himself between a flight of enemy bombers below and a flight of fighters above. As both flights began firing on him, the pilot snapped his fully loaded transport over into a roll, diving the plane on its back into the clouds to escape.

But the enemy also tried to use the weather to his own advantage in various ways. Late in 1942, for example, a number of ATC planes setting down through the weather over northern Burma on instruments crashed into the mountains for no explainable reason. Since its radio operators often monitored the traffic between the Assam bases and incoming aircraft, OSS Detachment 101 based at Fort Hertz, the lone Allied outpost in upper Burma, was able to pinpoint two

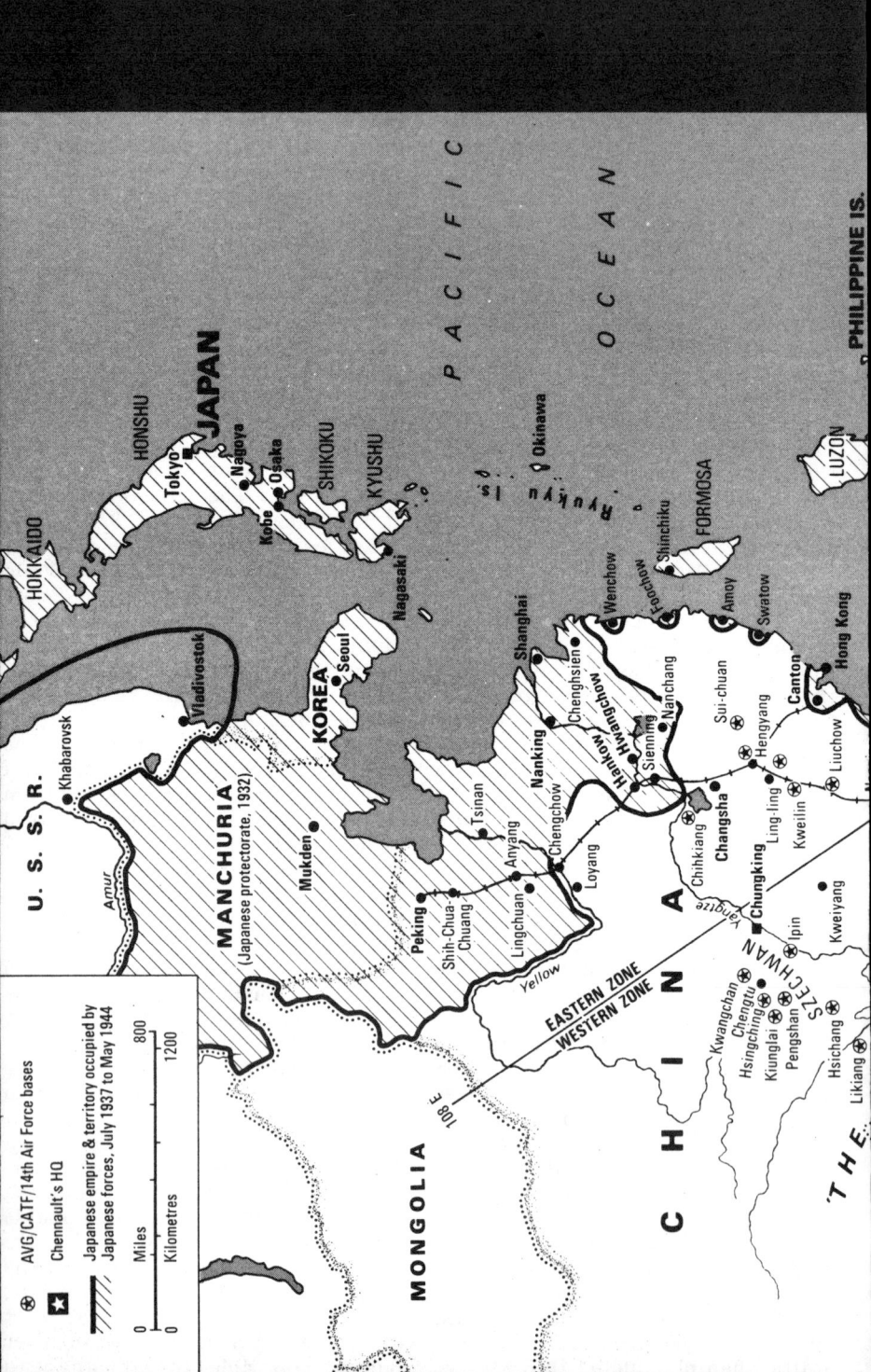

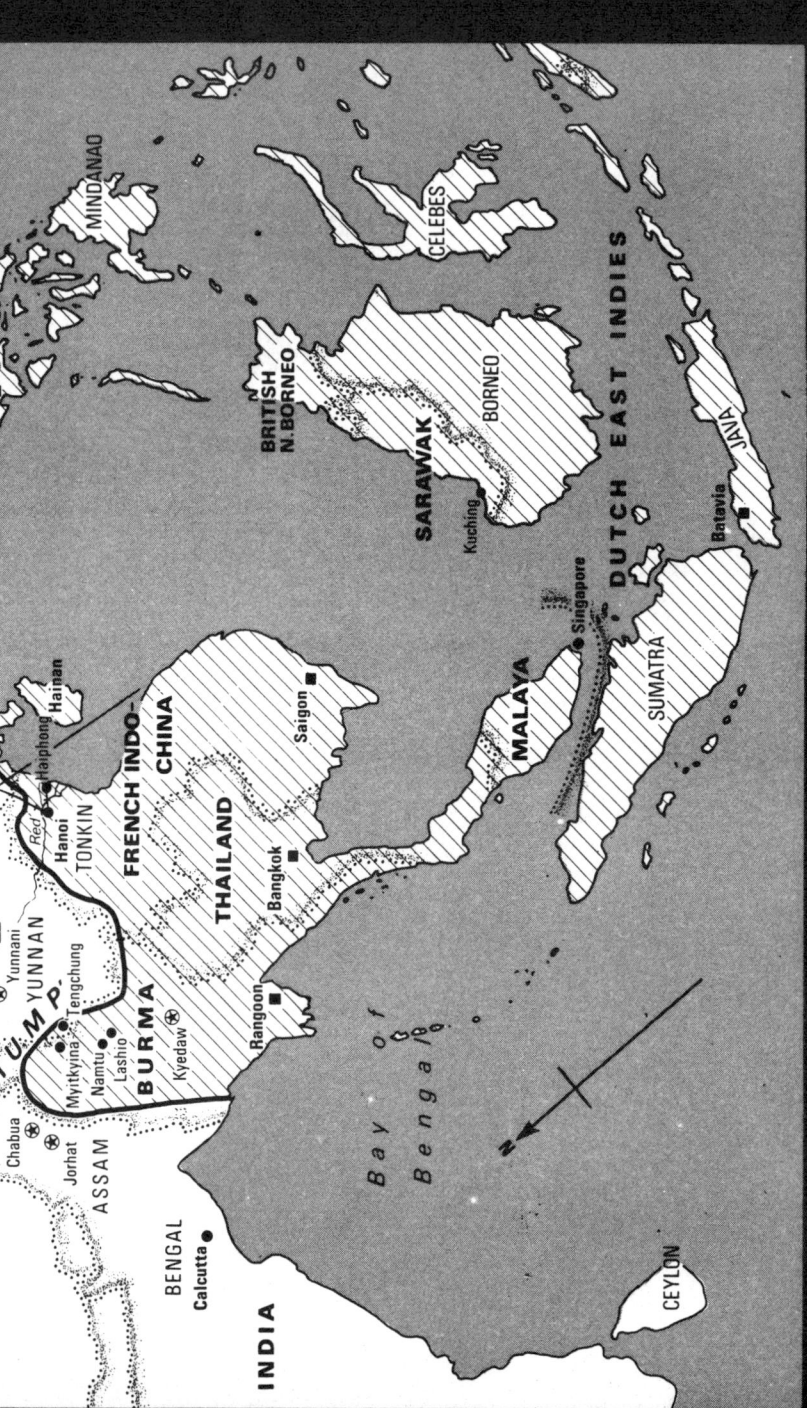

Chennault's bases (AVG, later CATF and 14th Air Force) in China

Above: Drums of aviation gasoline on their way over the hump to Chennault
Below: Chabua airdrome, one of the main ATC terminals in Assam

stations which were operating on the correct frequency but were seemingly located in the wrong places. Pilots fighting weather were glad to lock on to the DF or homing signals of these stations to guide them in. Further investigation revealed two cleverly operated Japanese deception stations so located that planes homing in on them crashed in nearby mountains. ATC changed its frequencies and the crashes ceased.

The high altitude flying over the hump created problems with certain kinds of cargo. For example, the standard Indian-made fifty-two gallon gasoline drum, normally loaded twenty-three to the plane, was strong enough in normal atmospheric pressure but burst regularly at 20,000 feet. In dealing with this kind of problem, the AAF found a valuable reservoir of experience in Pan American Airlines from its operations in the Andes. The same Pan Am studies of high altitude flying which made possible its high altitude freight runs in the Andes contributed valuable information to the India-China Wing of ATC.

Not only the weather over the hump but the weather in Assam presented problems for ATC. During the monsoon period between May and October, a rainfall of 200 inches or more is common in Assam. Thus, for six months of the year, only airdromes with paved runways and hardstandings can be used by any aircraft. Throughout 1942, the only such all-weather field was Dinjan, the others being seas of mud half the year. During the rainy season, Dinjan remained open to traffic until water became more than nine inches deep on the runways, at which point the field was closed for draining purposes. Alexander notes again: 'It has rained seven and a half inches in the past five days. All aircraft are grounded.'

At other times, heavy ground fogs fifteen feet deep enveloped the Assam bases, causing numerous crashes which did not help morale among the air crews. One night in 1943, the fog-bound ATC base at Chabua was circled by thirty transports seeking to land, all sending desperate signals for clearance. One of the old hump veterans, Captain Hugh Wild, took over as operations control officer in the tower and began talking the planes in. His record was creditable: eighteen landed safely, seven crashed while landing, and five were abandoned in the air when they ran out of gas. Wild was killed several days later when a downdraft blew his plane into the side of a mountain.

Weather forecasting was never very successful in CBI. The Tenth Weather Squadron was stationed in Delhi to assist the hump operations but was very short-staffed. At Kunming, one officer and six enlisted men had to rely on data collected by the Chinese air warning net which was intended to spot enemy planes rather than report weather. Even the B-29s staging out of India and China in 1944 as Project MATTERHORN had to use weather planes – fully armed B-29s – to fly ahead to send back last minute weather observations on the route and target area.

Throughout the three years of the hump airlift, weather was the greatest single cause of fluctuations in the air traffic between India and China. Even in 1945 when earlier shortages of men, *matériel*, and experience had been largely overcome, a single storm over the hump cost ATC nine planes and thirty-one crewmen killed or missing. Flying under these conditions, pilots developed a fatigue similar to combat fatigue which caused some to break under the strain. Flying time on the hump run was counted as official combat flying time by the AAF. It is not surprising that through 1943, eighty per cent of the decorations given to the men of ATC went to the India-China Wing.

Equally as important as the crews were the planes flying the hump. Despite strenuous efforts, the AAF was unable to produce a successful

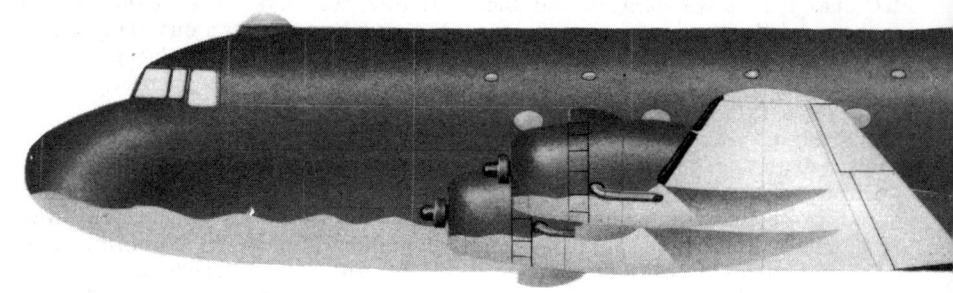

The US Douglas C-54 Skymaster transport and cargo carrier. Developed from the prewar triple-tailed DC-4 airliner, which was too big to meet US airlines' requirements, the C-54 was slightly smaller than its predecessor, and first flew in April 1942, by now fitted with a single fin and rudder. Large numbers were ordered before the end of the year, and it was considered important enough to warrant a factory devoted exclusively to its production. *Engines:* Four Pratt & Whitney R-2000 radials, 1,350hp each. *Accommodation:* Up to 42 passengers. *Speed:* 265mph. *Climb:* 1,350 feet per minute. *Ceiling:* 26,600 feet. *Range:* 3,800 miles maximum. *Weight empty/loaded:* 36,980/73,000lbs. *Span:* 117 feet 6 inches. *Length:* 93 feet 11 inches

design for a military transport during the war, hence had to turn to civilian transport models and modifications of its own heavy bombers. Aircraft models in use on the hump run at various times were the C-47, C-46, C-87 and C-54. With the exception of the C-87, these were all civilian transport models modified for military needs.

One of the most famous planes of the war, the C-47 was the first transport in service over the hump. Known as the Douglas DC-3 in its commercial models, the C-47 had been designed in 1935 and was already a standby of the airlines by 1938. A twin-engine monoplane, the C-47 had a 7,500-lb cargo capacity or could carry twenty-eight fully equipped troops, although it was known to have carried up to seventy-four during the evacuation of Burma. Although it had many features ill-suited to handling bulky cargo and too small a payload, the C-47 was flyable under almost any conditions, was easily maintained and, most importantly, was already in production. Since less was known about aeronautical engineering in 1935, the C-47 had been over-designed and hence was exceptionally durable. The AAF

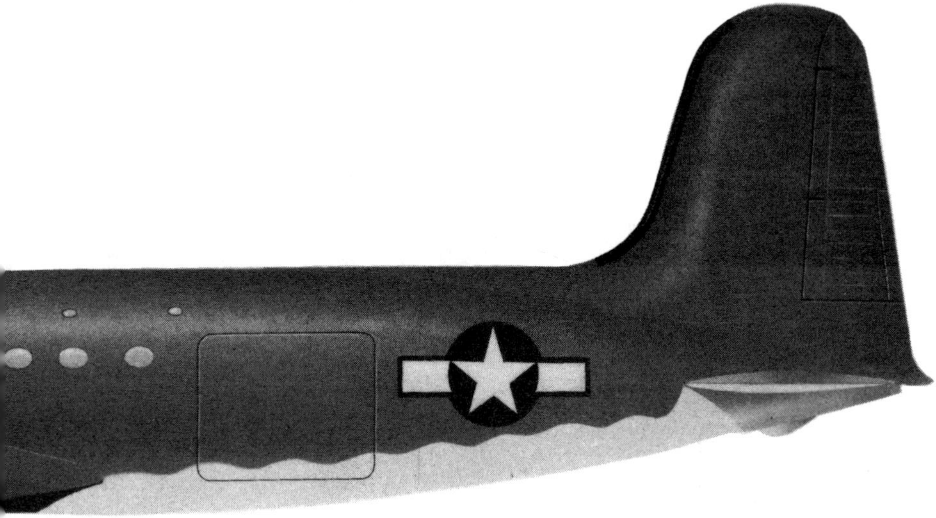

The C-54 could not be used on the northern hump route because of its low ceiling

The Consolidated B-24J Liberator. The H model of the B-24 was the first variant to be equipped with a nose turret and a retractable belly turret, shown to be necessary by the increased number of fighters encountered over Axis territory. The J model was essentially similar. Main points of difference were the outward opening nose wheel doors and the Motor Products nose turret. 6,728 B-24J's were built. *Engines:* Four Pratt & Whitney R-1830 radials, 1,200hp each at 25,000 feet. *Crew:* 9-11. *Armament:* Ten .5-inch Browning machine guns with 4,700 rounds and 5,000lbs of bombs carried internally (a maximum of 12,800lbs could be carried over very short distances). *Speed:* 300mph at 30,000 feet. *Climb:* 20,000 feet in 25 minutes. *Ceiling:* 28,000 feet. *Range:* 2,100 miles with ordinary bombload, 3,700 miles maximum. *Weight empty/loaded:* 36,500/65,000lbs. *Span:* 110 feet. *Length:* 67 feet 2 inches

purchased 10,000 C-47s between 1940 and 1945 – almost half of its transport fleet.

Desperate for transports early in the war, the AAF made over a number of four-engine B-24 bombers into transports, designating these planes C-87s. A special tanker model of the B-24 was known as the C-109 and used extensively on the hump run. Although there were many disadvantages to a made-over tactical plane, the C-87 filled the need for a long range four engine transport until the C-54 came into extensive use. The C-54 or Douglas

DC-4 was a four-engine transport just going into production at the beginning of the war. It became the workhorse of the AAF where long range and heavy payload were needed. The C-54 unfortunately had a low ceiling, so could not be used on the northern hump route and did not see service in the airlift until the southern route was reopened in 1944. The AAF had 1,000 C-54s by 1945.

In 1943, the C-46 made its appearance as the military version of an unproven Curtiss-Wright commercial transport. Like the C-47, the C-46 was a twin-

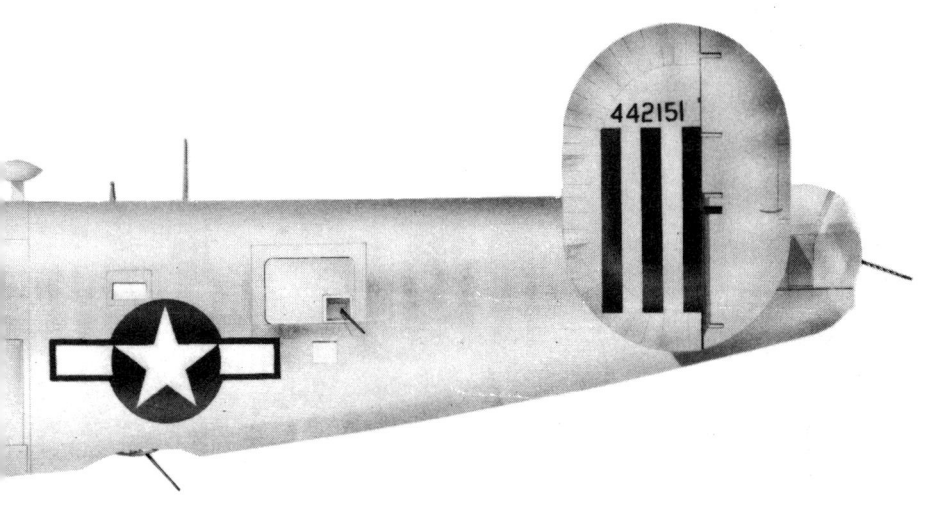

engine monoplane but larger, heavier, and more powerful with a cargo capacity thirty-three per cent greater than its Douglas competitor. The C-46 was easy to load, had good lift, speed and range but was hard to fly and maintain. Pressed into service before it had been thoroughly flight-tested, it was subject to various mechanical ailments which quickly became apparent on the hump, the most difficult of all ATC routes. Particular problems were failures in the gas transfer systems, undependable engines, and lack of defrosters on carburetors. All C-46s sent to CBI required numerous time-consuming modifications which were difficult to perform at ATC's Indian maintenance depots. Known as the 'flying coffin' because of its tendency to blow up or crash, the C-46 was initially considered by ATC pilots as a menace equal to the hump weather and terrain. After its engineering problems were solved, however, the C-46 came into extensive use in 1944 and gradually replaced the C-47 as the workhorse of CBI. The AAF purchased a total of 3,144 C-46s by 1945.

For three years, every vehicle, gallon of gasoline, round of ammunition, ream of paper, and other supplies which China received were flown in by these planes. Jeeps, 6 × 6 trucks, ambulances, P-40 wing panels, aircraft engines, troops, PX supplies, mail, clothing, and rations were other items often aboard as cargo. On the return trips, mail, engines for overhaul, personnel, and raw materials such as tungsten and hog bristles were carried.

The hump operations were severely limited by a lack of planes until mid-1943 but an equally limiting factor was keeping the planes on hand in service. Maintenance remained a critical problem for ATC until 1945. Service units in CBI were always spread extremely thinly, hence policy in the theater was to request that air service units accompany new tactical or transport groups. The Tenth Air Service Command was the agency

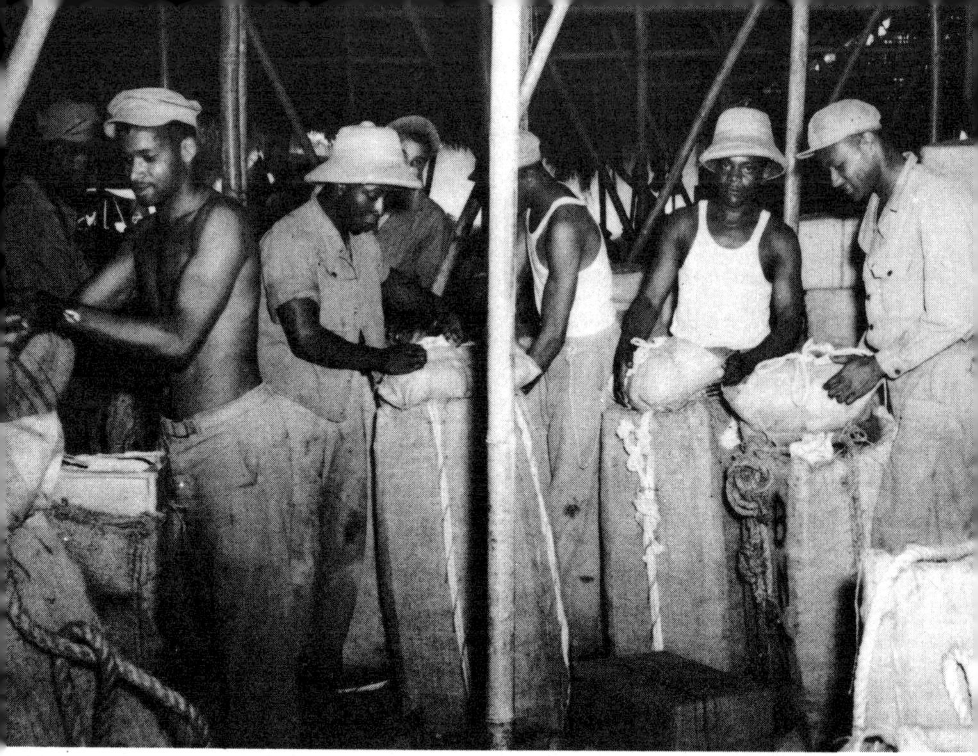

Above: Quartermaster troops pack articles in layers of rice husks to protect them during air transport. *Below:* After going over the hump to Yunnan, supplies are packed by Chinese workers for air drop to Chinese troops

Above: Dismantled for the flight over the hump, construction equipment and trucks are reassembled in Yunnan. *Below:* A 2,000lb B-25 engine is loaded at Kunming for a flight to India and overhaul

The C-109 was the tanker model of the C-87 and was used extensively over the hump

responsible for the procurement of supplies and the maintenance and repair of all CBI aircraft. Working closely with the Army Services of Supply, the Air Service Command obtained and transported Tenth Air Force supplies and repaired, overhauled, salvaged, and manufactured aircraft. Headquartered at Hastings Mill near Calcutta, the Air Service Command had two special repair depots. Bangaore serviced C-47s, C-87s and C-109s while Agra serviced C-46s and the overflow of C-47s from Bangalore. Early a vital component of the Air Service Command's maintenance system, Bangalore was the home of the Hindustan Aircraft Corporation, owned by the Government of India and Mysore. Bangalore not only manufactured and repaired planes for its owners but undertook a contract to build fifty single-engine Vultees for the Chinese government. In August 1942, the Air Service Command was able to obtain the services of the best aircraft facility in India when the Hindustan Aircraft Corporation agreed to service, repair, overhaul, and fabricate all necessary parts of American produced aircraft engines.

Other problems for maintenance were the extreme heat, high humidity, and dust. Maintenance work was normally carried out at night because, as Alexander reported: 'Maintenance work cannot be accomplished because shade temperatures of from 100° to 150° Fahrenheit render all metal exposed to the sun so hot that it cannot be touched by the human hand without causing second degree burns.' The humidity produced a great deal of rot and rust while the thick dust in Assam during the dry season caused far greater engine wear than was normal, necessitating more frequent overhauls. Service crews faced other hazards as well. One crew chief came hurtling out of a plane, screaming, 'There's a cobra in there!' At a loss as to how to proceed, the Americans called in their British colleagues who in turn consulted some Indian civil servants. The Indians produced a mongoose which was locked in the

plane. The mongoose emerged snakeless but three missions later the frozen body of a cobra was found behind some ammunition boxes in the waist.

By far the most serious problem of maintenance was the chronic lack of spare parts and engines. The Air Service Command normally expected four per cent of CBI aircraft to be out of commission for lack of parts. When the figure reached more than four per cent, a condition of critical scarcity was considered to exist. By this standard, January 1945 was the first month in which such a condition did not exist. For example, 1944 showed a monthly average of 5.3 per cent of aircraft out of commission for lack of parts. In 1942, the spare parts problem was the key factor in limiting the hump. Only nine of the thirty-four transports assigned to the hump run in June were actually flyable, the rest grounded for want of parts. Towards the end of 1943, almost 100 transports of the hump fleet were grounded at one point.

In concert with other attempts to increase the hump lift in the summer of 1943, the ATC Commander, General

A C-87. On the Fireball Express run they were stripped of camouflage paint to give an extra five mph air speed

Harold George, instituted the 'Fireball Express' in recognition of the fact that nothing was more vital to the expansion of the lift than an adequate flow of parts and engines. Operating under ATC contract, Pan Am crews made a weekly flight to carry the parts in most demand direct from the Air Service Command Depot at Fairfield, Ohio to the Tenth Air Service Command Depot at Agra. Flying C-87s stripped of camouflage paint to give them an extra 5mph airspeed, the express crews used the Florida-Brazil-West Africa-Sudan route to India, making the round trip in seven days. The increased flow of parts added greatly to the number of aircraft in service on the hump run.

Although the shortages of planes and parts were major factors in limiting the hump lift, overall the most critical factor was the initial lack of all-weather airdromes and the slow progress in construction of new fields. As the only all-weather field in

**Sir Archibald Wavell, Governor-General
and Viceroy of India**

Assam in 1942, Dinjan was saturated
with RAF, CNAC, and Tenth Air
Force planes. Construction of new
facilities was the responsibility of the
Indian Government and Army, of
which the United States had requested
thirty-four airfields and supporting
installations. Construction was thus
underway on fields at Jorhat, Mohanbari, Sookerating, Chabua, and Tezgaon.

Having only local labor and materials available, the British were en-
countering many problems with the
airfield program. The labor force was
primarily women who often refused
to work in the rain or were absent on
numerous religious holidays. No heavy
construction equipment was available
so the work was carried on by hand
and basket. As Japanese propaganda
intensified and fear of a Japanese
invasion grew among the Indians, the
native labor force in Assam, the most

exposed part of India, melted away at
an alarming rate in the spring of 1942.
Promises of American labor troops
and heavy machinery went unfulfilled.
The airdrome construction program
fell far behind schedule, so far that
Brereton complained strongly to the
British commander, Sir Archibald
Wavell, that the airdrome program
was not being pushed, that native labor
for Assam was not being assembled,
and that 'the ever present red tape of
the Indian Civil Service' was compli-
cating matters generally. The airdrome program was not a priority concern of the British Command because
it did not share American enthusiasm
for China's potential role in the war.
Thus Brereton's complaint was to be
echoed frequently by other American
commanders until mid-1943 when both
Roosevelt and Churchill put their
authority directly behind the program
in recognition of the fact that the
hump lift could not be increased sub-
stantially until the new bases were
completed.

The situation was not critical at
the China terminal of the hump route.
The Kunming airdrome was able to
handle its traffic without much difficulty. Lying 6,000 feet above sea level
on the Yunnan plateau, the airdrome
was a rough strip cut out of red clay.
Originally rice paddies, the field had
been built by coolies who scooped out
by hand a trench 6,000 feet long, 100
feet wide, and four feet deep, filled it
with large rocks, then smaller rocks,
and finally packed it with gravel and
clay. When dry, the field was pink and
brick-like but wet, it was slick red
mud and jagged stones. But although
it was primitive, it had been the chief
airfield of unoccupied China since 1938
and supported heavy bombers and
transports. When increasing traffic
by ATC and Chennault's Fourteenth
Air Force created a need for more
airdromes, Chiang Kai-shek did not
hesitate to put hundreds of thousands
of coolies to work to build the needed
facilities. Airdromes in China never
constituted a problem of the magni-

Above: The labor force building the Assam airdromes was primarily composed of women. *Below:* Work was carried on by hand and basket since no heavy construction equipment was available

tude faced by the Tenth Air Force and ATC in India.

India was a poor base for the supply effort to relieve China for two reasons. An agricultural land with a population of 400,000,000 already on the verge of famine, India had no surplus capacity for military effort and hence was not an important source of the supplies required in China, most of which had to be brought to India by water or air. Thus Indian contributions to the war effort generally represented sacrifices on the part of a people who had not enough for themselves. For Americans, India represented a difficult environment in which to carry on the effort to relieve China. Troops suffered severely from disease in an area where smallpox, plague, malaria, and intestinal problems are endemic. Local food generally was poor and limited in

Chiang Kai-shek put thousands of laborers to work building the new airdromes needed by ATC and Chennault

variety. Soldiers lost weight and grew tired and listless from vitamin deficiency. The difficulty of obtaining fresh food in Assam made it worthwhile on occasion to fly perishables from China to India. The ever present heat and alternating dust and rain of Assam were wearing on American troops. In these circumstances. the medical services had to keep close watch on the physical condition of the soldiers since the possibility of mass debilitation was very real. Whole units are on record as being unable to function as a result of disease. general debilitation or both.

India was also in political turmoil in 1942. Encouraged by Japanese and German propaganda and British reverses in Europe, the Indian nationalist movement led by Mahatma Gandhi was fighting for political autonomy. The failure of the mission led by Sir Stafford Cripps in early 1942 had led to an impasse between the nationalists and the Indian government. Widespread civil strife was

As in Assam, airdromes in China were built largely by hand

imminent. On 9th August, Gandhi was arrested, igniting serious riots, strikes, and sabotage which halted many of the construction projects vital to the hump build-up. The American Command took every precaution to prevent sabotage and to keep its troops from being involved, even to the extent of restricting them to their bases when it was deemed necessary. Dependent on the Indian Government for facilities and transportation, the Americans were in an ambiguous position. On one hand, they were viewed with some ambivalence by the Indian government which saw them as one more factor to complicate the already complex and unstable situation in the country. On the other hand, they were viewed with suspicion by Gandhi who feared that the Americans were there mainly to support

The leader of the Indian nationalist movement, Mahatma Gandhi, enters the Viceroy's house in Delhi for conversations with Sir Stafford Cripps

Sir Stafford Cripps. He failed to reach an accommodation with the Indian nationalists in early 1942

British rule in India.

Moving supplies to China actually constituted only one part of the problem of the hump lift. The other part was to get the supplies from the United States to the Assam terminals of the hump route. India lay at the end of a 12,000 mile long supply line, the longest supply line of the war and one which, in 1942, was subject to the uncertain prospects of the British forces in North Africa and the Middle East. Convoys took two months or more to make the 12,000-mile voyage from American ports. Since eastern India was subject to Japanese air attacks in 1942-1943, supplies had to be debarked at west Indian ports, thus necessitating an additional haul of 1,500 miles trans-India to Assam.

The question of a port of entry for American supplies was a difficult one in 1942. Bombay was considered to be

69

the best port in India but, as an American report noted, was 'hopelessly clogged with mismanaged Allied shipping'. Calcutta was an excellent port and the obvious choice to support the Assam bases but was exposed to enemy air attack and hence unusable. Karachi was thus selected as the American port of entry, leaving Bombay to the British. Karachi had adequate water, hospital, and other facilities. Its only drawback was that it lay separated from Assam by the width of India, a matter of some 1,500 miles.

The Indian transportation system was wholly inadequate for moving large quantities of *matériel* from Karachi to Assam. The road system was simply undeveloped, hence motor transport could not be seriously considered, even if trucks had been in sufficient supply. The burden therefore fell on the rail system which had

already been weakened by the transfer of rolling stock and locomotives to Iran, hence was unable to absorb the additional traffic of the Americans without numerous delays and breakdowns.

A broad gauge line, double tracked part of the way, ran from Karachi to Delhi while another line connected Delhi with the area north of Calcutta. Service was slow but these lines did not constitute the main problem. The real bottleneck on the trip between Karachi and Assam was the Assam-Bengal Railroad which had two different gauges of track and a combination of barge and rail connections, all of which required periodic transshipments of cargo by physically weak native labor. Running up the Brahmaputra river valley, the line had been built to market the Assam tea crop. The management of the line found it difficult to cope with the sudden increase in trains from three to fourteen a day. Transshipment facilities designed for the tea crop were hopelessly

Survivors of a search and rescue C-47 shot down by the Japanese

inadequate for war *matériel*. There were no bridges over the Brahmaputra, hence ferries had to be used. It took supplies two months to come the 12,000 miles from the United States to Karachi and six weeks to complete the 1,500-mile trip to Assam. It is therefore hardly surprising that Brereton and Naiden felt it necessary to set up a trans-India air ferry service at the same time they were initiating the Assam-Burma-China ferry.

Crews of planes flying the hump were in constant danger of being shot down by enemy fighters or forced down by weather over rugged jungle and mountain terrain in upper Burma. Some were killed landing, some captured by the enemy, while the remainder usually became lost and died of starvation in the jungle. ATC could ill afford to lose the personnel but rescue attempts were not seriously contemplated until early 1943 when OSS Detachment 101 offered the services of its guerrillas in upper Burma in return for planes and para-

chutes. At that time, Detachment 101 was building a force of 10,000 Kachin guerrillas and thus had an extensive network of agents and contacts among the hill people. ATC was glad to co-operate since it helped the morale of its crews to know that there was at least a chance of assistance from Allied agents and friendly natives. Units of 101 operating in north Burma rescued over 125 airmen. At one point, the 101 Station at Fort Hertz was so crowded with rescued airmen that extra food and medical personnel had to be flown in. It is estimated that 101 rescued twenty-five per cent of the airmen downed over north Burma. Sometimes 101 personnel arrived too late to do anything but record the gruesome fate imposed by the jungle on downed airmen. In several cases, airmen had parachuted into a tall tree, 100-150 feet high, with the result that their bodies went through but their parachutes caught in the branches. Often hurt, they hung suspended in the jump harness 100 feet off the

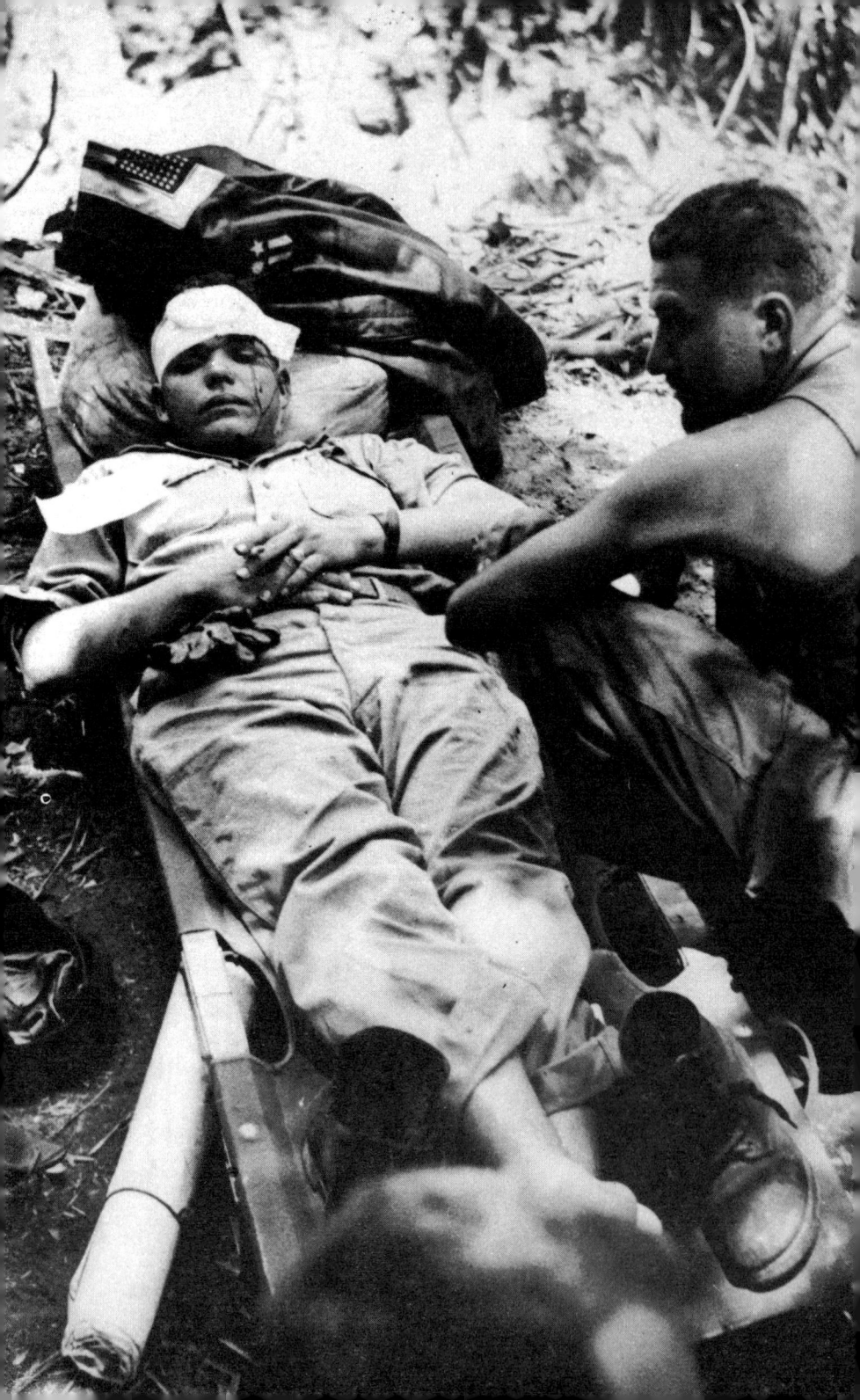

ground, able neither to climb up nor drop down and thus died an agonizing death. By the time the rescuers arrived, ants had eaten away their flesh: all that remained was a skeleton hanging in a tree.

101 also ran a course in jungle survival training for ATC personnel, most of whom lived a military life remote from the jungle and thus had to be taught from the start. Though familiar with an airplane compass, many could not use a hand compass. Instead of following streams downhill to civilization, 101 taught ATC personnel to go upstream away from the Japanese occupied lowlands to the highlands, habitat of the friendly Kachins, where assistance could be found. As part of the course, airmen had to live two weeks in the jungle with rations, survival tools, and a blanket. Crew chiefs were trained first and in turn trained their own men, so that within a short time, most of the crews flying the hump had received this course which gave them confidence and lifted morale.

As the India-China Wing began to expand in the spring of 1943, ATC Intelligence officers concentrated on collecting scattered details about the natives, terrain, paths, food, Japanese patrol positions, and other information to aid downed flyers. Airmen rescued by 101 were intensively debriefed and yielded valuable information about hitherto uncharted country. Revised maps and information about the inhabitants, friendly and unfriendly; American, British, and Chinese outposts; and river and overland routes, were made available to all flying personnel. In October 1943, search and rescue work was consolidated in the Air Search and Rescue Unit, the duties of which were to search for downed planes, identify and pinpoint all wrecks, aid downed personnel in remote areas, and maintain close communication with all

The pilot of a downed C-47 awaits evacuation from north Burma

possible sources of information such as Intelligence units, ground units, missionaries, and civil officers. With several planes of their own, Search and Rescue personnel flew search missions and dropped supplies and instructions to survivors of crashes. In emergencies, medical personnel parachuted in to aid wounded survivors on the long walk home. A representative search and rescue mission occurred in September 1943 when a C-47 crashed in north Burma. The one badly burned survivor was carried by friendly Kachins sixteen miles to the nearest British outpost, an arduous trip requiring nine days. A two man rescue team hiked in fifty miles, called for an airdrop of medical supplies, nursed the wounded survivor for a month, after which all three walked out. The longest walkout on record occurred when a crew of four spent ninety-three days in the jungle.

The year 1942 was a particularly difficult one for the Tenth Air Force in that it had many problems to overcome but few resources with which to work. This was also true in the sphere of defense, as overshadowing the other problems of launching the hump lift was the threat of Japanese attack. Having completely isolated China by land and sea, it was expected that the enemy would now try to close the air route as well. In the summer of 1942 the Japanese had an estimated 167 planes based in Burma and more available from bases in Thailand and French Indo-China. Already Japanese fighters were making sweeps over north Burma in search of the unarmed transports flying the hump. The Tenth Air Force expected raids on its Assam and China bases when the monsoon lifted in the fall.

The airlift was vulnerable at its Indian and Chinese terminals and where its route crossed over north Burma. The defense of the airlift was divided between the China Air Task Force (CATF) under Chennault and the India Air Task Force (IATF) under Brigadier-General Caleb Haynes.

General Claire Chennault talks with some CATF fighter pilots in China

General Caleb Haines, commander of the IATF which defended the Assam end of the hump route

With an air task force at either end, Stilwell and Bissell felt the hump route could be operated in some security. The CATF had been activated on 7th July and comprised the remnants of Chennault's American Volunteer Group augmented by some regular AAF personnel. At that time, the CATF had its main base at Kunming and had fifty-six P-40s and eight B-25s as its striking force. The primary mission of the CATF was to defend the southern and eastern approaches of the hump route and its China terminals while its secondary mission was to destroy hostile aircraft and provide air support for Chinese troops. To protect the hump, the CATF sent strikes against the Japanese bases at Lashio, Loiwing, Bhamo, and Myitkyina whenever intelligence reported the enemy staging planes in these areas. In 1938, Chennault had built a highly effective air warning net to protect his bases and planes from surprise attacks by the superior enemy forces. The warning net and intercepts of Japanese code messages which the Chinese had broken enabled Chennault to operate his tiny air force against vast numerical odds as he often knew where the enemy was going to strike in time to concentrate his forces. Japanese air attacks were usually intercepted well before they reached CATF bases.

Activated in October 1942, the IATF had nine squadrons on paper, none of which were fully prepared for combat. There were four heavy bomber squadrons, one of which was still in the Middle East, one just receiving its planes, and two still only cadres; three medium bomber squadrons, two of which were still without aircraft; and two fighter squadrons, one operational at Dinjan and one in training at Karachi. Because the CATF required a large number of fighters but only a few bombers, the IATF had obviously been left badly balanced in the division of aircraft between the two. The geography of CBI and the nature of enemy deployment also left the IATF with far the greater responsibility for the defense of the hump.

Unlike the well defended China terminals, the Assam installations of the India-China Ferry were essentially defenseless in the fall of 1942. There were no anti-aircraft batteries and only one fighter squadron but the main need was for an air warning system since Japanese planes were based within three hours flying time in Burma. A radar net was impossible because of the high mountains nearby. Naiden therefore had to resort to stationing small detachments with light radios and portable generators in the hills east of Assam. He also tried to enlist the aid of the natives as had Chennault in China but because of the great area that had to be covered, the whole system was simply ineffective. Planes could easily slip through without observation while those sighted were over their target by the time the warning message was received. At the least, more radio detachments were needed but despite repeated appeals to Washington, Brereton and Naiden could not obtain them. Bissell enlisted Stilwell's aid by convincing him that Assam was in grave danger, which it was, but even the result of Stilwell's intervention was only five more radio teams which did not arrive until the following March, shortly before the onset of the next monsoon. Thus until the fall, the real defense of the Assam bases consisted of the protective cover of the monsoon.

In September, various signs indicated that the enemy was preparing heavy blows against the hump terminals in Assam and China. Air reconnaissance reported a sudden increase in fighter strength around Hanoi, indicating that staging operations between Formosa and Burma were under way. On 3rd October, Chennault radioed Bissell: 'Possibility enemy air attack on Dinjan other bases supporting ferry route in India stop Kunming and western Yunnan bases as well as ferry route itself.' As a preventive measure, the CATF sent a strike against Gia Lam airfield at Hanoi which destroyed seventeen enemy fighters on the ground.

On 25th October, simultaneous assaults were launched against Kunming and Assam as predicted by Chennault. Alerted by its warning net, the CATF met and turned back a force of Japanese bombers and fighters 100 miles south of Kunming. With obvious full knowledge of conditions in Assam, 100 Japanese bombers and fighters struck Dinjan, Mohanbari, Chabua, and Sookerating but only the important airdromes at Dinjan and Chabua were heavily bombed. The attack caused severe damage to runways and buildings, destroyed five transports and seven fighters on the ground, and damaged four other transports and thirteen fighters. Three American fighters happened to be airborne, six others managed to take off, but the defense was token. The attackers had appeared over the bases as the warning was being received from the detection stations. A second attack by fifty bombers and fighters the following day concentrated on Sook-

erating. No warning was received and no interception was made. A third raid on 28th October caused light damage and was thought to have been primarily for reconnaissance purposes.

After the raids, all available fighters in India were rushed to Assam along with some anti-aircraft batteries but the warning system could not be improved without additional men and equipment. Bissell used the occasion to repeat his request for more equipment and the return of the Tenth Air Force units still in the Middle East. Had the Japanese pressed their attacks, they might very well have destroyed the Assam end of the hump route but the raids ceased after October in favor of strikes on shipping and dock areas at Calcutta and Chittagong and the Indian airdromes of Dum Dum, Alipore, and Fenny. Although later raids were again directed at Assam, the Japanese would never again have such an opportunity to strike at the vitals of the India-China ferry. By January 1943 the IATF was fully organized with all squadrons operational though not at full strength. The IATF was now ready to challenge the Japanese for air supremacy over Burma – a challenge which, if successful, would allow the hump transports and bases to operate in complete security.

Born only as measure of desperate necessity, the India-China airlift had been beset with insurmountable problems during the first nine months of its operation. Roosevelt's promises to Chiang Kai-shek in early 1942 had required a relatively modest tonnage – only 3,500 tons per month – but the airlift had yet to achieve even half of that goal as it entered 1943 under the new management of ATC. And as ATC began to struggle with the same problems as had its predecessor the Tenth Air Force, the Allied heads of state ordered the men and planes of the airlift, to that point a rather dismal failure, to reach a new and even more impossible goal as the American commitment to China was increased.

Sookerating airdrome in Assam, an all-weather field with a 6,000-foot concrete runway

New commitments

Marshal Sir John Dill, Generals
Chennault, Arnold, Stilwell, and
Bissell at the January 1943 meeting
with Chiang Kai-shek in Chungking

In addition to its other problems with the hump, the India-China Wing of ATC was faced with the recurrent promises made by Roosevelt to China for ever higher tonnage. Shortly after ATC was given responsibility for the hump lift in December 1942, new commitments were being made by Roosevelt to Chiang Kai-shek as a result of the Casablanca Conference. Thus the story of the hump was now to have another dimension, that of trying to meet ever-rising quotas set by others who were governed by political considerations rather than the logistic realities of CBI.

By the beginning of 1943, two major conflicts with great significance for the airlift had become apparent in CBI. A serious clash in war aims between the British and Chinese was evident which in turn produced a divergence between American and British goals. Within the American command, there were also two schools of strategy about the best means to pursue American war aims. This led to a struggle for control of the available resources in CBI since the Allies did not possess enough to support both efforts. Since any action depended on the cooperation of the British and Chinese, these were drawn into the internal conflict among the Americans. Thus the diplomacy surrounding the direction of the war in CBI became quite complex and revolved around four conferences held by the Allies to discuss war policies during 1943. These conferences – Casablanca, Trident, Quadrant, and Sextant – were the stage on which the various conflicts within CBI were played out and as such became the determining influence on the success or failure of the air route to China.

The conflict between British and Chinese interests was that of an imperial power versus a colonized country struggling for its integrity. Britain had, after all, been the original violator of China's sovereignty and founder of the hated unequal treaties which were still in force. The closing of the

Roosevelt and Churchill confer at the
Casablanca Conference in December
1942

Burma Road in 1940 had been bitterly resented by the Chinese who also correctly feared that the British were pre-empting China's share of lend-lease. For their part, the British held little respect for China's government or military capacity and minimized her value in the war. As early as the Arcadia Conference of 1941, Churchill had told Roosevelt that he was 'over-estimating China's potential contribution'. Once Burma had fallen, Britain had no other interest than that the imperial territories be regained after the war. The British were thus unsympathetic to the American preoccupation with breaking the blockade of China. The Anglo-American split was a recurrent theme in the conferences of 1943.

In addition to disagreeing on China's role in the war, the Americans and British had different views of China's postwar status as well. One of Roosevelt's governing ideas was that China must fill the vacuum in Asia left by the defeat of Japan and must therefore be treated as a great power. His war aims were thus not only the defeat of Japan but to build up China for her postwar role as great power. Churchill did not want a strong China which could challenge Britain's position in Asia after the war. The Chinese would certainly try to regain Hong Kong and had old imperial claims on Tibet and north Burma. As Ambassador John Winant remarked to another American official during the Quadrant conference, 'The PM is quite willing to see China collapse'. The Anglo-American split over China stunted strategic planning in CBI and is one reason why major operations in the theater did not get under way until 1944.

Chiang Kai-shek, however, had every intention of emerging on the winning side and still at the helm of his country. From the beginning, he played a skill-ful game of extracting maximum support from the Americans in return for minimum contribution by his forces. Like Churchill, he believed that Japan would be defeated else-where and was primarily concerned with building up his forces for the post-war confrontation which both he and his communist opponents knew was inevitable. Since he had nothing to gain from the Japanese and had already rebuffed various Japanese overtures, the chronic American fear of a separate peace between Chiang and the Japanese contained an element of unreality but was kept alive by Chiang through frequent and fervent cries of impending collapse. China thus became America's special burden – a burden compounded of guilt for past injustices and failures, guardianship of a weak ally in need, and illusion of a strong China after the war.

The diplomacy of 1943 opened at the Allied conference in Casablanca in December. Roosevelt, Churchill and the Combined Chiefs of Staff were all present on this occasion. Absent were Stalin, who declined due to the military situation in the Soviet Union, and Chiang Kai-shek, who had not been invited even though he was the supreme commander of the China Theater. The conference was a thorough survey of the war theater by theater and resulted in little change in the strategic concept for the employment of allied troops and resources. The major effort was still to be directed against Germany with second priority to a two pronged offensive from the central and south-west Pacific toward Japan.

Lowest priority still went to CBI but at Casablanca came the first formal discussion among the Allies of the competing strategies for that theater, proposed by Generals Stil-well and Chennault. Under develop-ment since his now-famous trek out of Burma in May 1942, Stilwell's plan was to assemble and train 45,000 Chinese troops at Ramgarh in India as

Following the Casablanca Conference, Churchill and Roosevelt met again at Marrakech in French Morocco

General Stilwell, who spoke excellent Chinese, addresses troops of the Chinese Thirty-Eighth Army training at Ramgarh, India

his X force and a further twenty-seven divisions of Chinese troops in Yunnan as his Y force. In a pincer movement, the X force would advance south-eastwards from Ledo in Assam building a road behind it until it linked up with a similar advance by the Y force from Yunnan, thus forcing the enemy out of northern Burma and restoring land communications between China and Assam. Concurrent British operations against Rangoon and up the Irrawaddy valley would meet a southward drive by the Chinese forces, thus clearing all of Burma and opening the port of Rangoon. Stilwell believed that the enemy must be driven from Burma as a necessary prerequisite to the establishment of air bases in China from which Japan's

sea communications and home islands could be bombed. The role of the airlift in this plan was to fly enough lend-lease to China to equip the Y force.

A brilliant tactician and advocate of air power, Chennault countered that the reconquest of Burma and the building of the Ledo Road would prolong the war by using men and material better employed in building airfields in Assam and China. He believed that the Japanese position in China was vulnerable to air attack because the occupied areas and the sea communications on which the Japanese depended were equally accessible to central China where the CATF was deployed. With 500 planes, Chennault thought it possible to destroy the Japanese air force and enable the Allies to advance across the Pacific without fear of land-based aviation. He, too, assumed that the hump could be adequately expanded to support his operations.

The Chief of Naval Operations, Admiral Ernest King, was a firm supporter of Stilwell

The Chief of Staff, General George Marshall. He was an old friend and also a firm supporter of Stilwell

The conflict was really over means since each plan led to the same end – the establishment of bases in China from which Japan could be bombed. Both strategies were receiving discussion in Washington and each had its supporters. The American Chief of Staff, General George Marshall, and the Chief of Naval Operations, Admiral Ernest King, were firmly supporting Stilwell, who had already begun preparations for his project, while General Arnold of the AAF held that 'the only intelligent move immediately is to strengthen Chennault's air force and get at the bombing of Japan as soon as possible.' With variations in detail, these two plans competed throughout 1943 although ultimately each was to have its day.

Codenamed ANAKIM, Stilwell's Burma campaign was approved by the Combined Chiefs of Staff at Casablanca as necessary to break the blockade of China and scheduled for the following November. The British were only lukewarm to ANAKIM and consented mainly because a final decision was not to be made until July. Not only the British but Roose-velt as well had doubts about ANAK-IM. In his mind, ground warfare was slow and costly as opposed to an air offensive which offered a quick and cheap way to damage the enemy. Whichever plan was selected made little difference for the airlift at this point as both required a major expansion.

The key factor in ANAKIM was participation by the Chinese whose agreement had not yet been obtained. A mission composed of General Arnold, General Brehon Somervell of the Army Services of Supply, and Marshal Sir John Dill of the British Staff Mission flew to China immediately after Casablanca to explain the Allies' global strategy to Chiang, to obtain his commitment to ANAKIM, and to smooth over the fact that he had not been invited to Casablanca. To balance Arnold's support of the air plan, Marshall had included Somervell, a representative of the army view that the airlift would never replace the Burma Road. By way of introduction to China's line of communications, the mission's plane, flown by a picked crew, became lost over the hump and

Generalissimo Chiang Kai-shek inspects Chinese troops on the north Burma front

arrived in Chungking four hours late.

As was the case in almost all matters pertaining to the China Theater, the discussions began and ended with the question of the airlift. Chiang's view was that China had been fighting six years and had received no assistance. In response to his proposals for more supplies, all he received was excuses from that 'old woman' Bissell about the problems of river traffic, the railroad in Assam, etc. In order for China to join in the proposed Burma campaign, three things were necessary. Firstly, there must be an independent air force under Chennault as Chiang had no confidence in Bissell. Secondly, the airlift must be increased to 10,000 tons per month as soon as possible. Thirdly, Chennault's air force must have 500 planes by November with no excuses about logistic problems. Like Roosevelt, Chiang saw the Chennault thesis as the answer because it promised quick results with no investment on his part.

Arnold replied that he would order the number of transports on the hump run raised from the present sixty-two to 137 with the aim of increasing the tonnage from 1,228 in December 1942 to 4,000 by April 1943. He said that the CATF would be increased to the extent that the hump lift would support it. The problem of supplying gas to the CATF planes was paramount as Arnold tried to convince Chiang and Chennault. For every gallon reaching China, six gallons had to come in through Karachi or Calcutta. Both Arnold and Dill felt that Chiang had a sharp mind but ignored facts and logistics while Chennault, excellent at working with the Chinese and conducting tactical operations, was weak in administration and oversimplified logistic problems. One result of the mission was Arnold's decision to send Chennault a contingent of staff officers to strengthen his command in these respects.

The mission had other results as well. In the end, Chiang agreed to participate in the Burma campaign but

reiterated that the hump tonnage was the weak spot in planning as his forces must have more supplies to participate. Through the Arnold-Somervell report, Roosevelt and the War Department received a vivid preliminary picture of the personality clashes which complicated the situation in CBI and were to come to a head at the Trident Conference a few months later. Stilwell and Bissell tended to be aligned against Chiang and Chennault with a good deal of personal enmity on both sides. This split reached back to Washington where Stilwell and Bissell were supported by the military establishment and Chiang and Chennault by various pro-China journalists and presidential assistants, most notably Harry Hop-

kins. Lastly, the Arnold mission was the first step toward prodding the airlift out of its doldrums and failure toward the dynamism which eventually enabled it to surpass the high goals set for it.

Already leaning toward the air offensive rather than ANAKIM, Roosevelt came under heavy Chinese pressure to make a decision favorable to Chennault. In October 1942 Chennault had conveyed his views directly to Roosevelt in a letter carried by Wendell Wilkie, then on a world tour. With 105 fighters, thirty medium and twelve heavy bombers, Chennault stated that the Japanese air force in China could be destroyed in six months to a year, after which Japan's sea communications and industrial cen-

Chiang Kai-shek fully supported Chennault's proposed air offensive and opposed Stilwell's plan for a Burma campaign

tres could be attacked. In order to have the necessary freedom of action, however, he must be able to report directly to Chiang. When released by Roosevelt, this letter caused a major scandal in the War Department and sent Chennault's standing with the military establishment even lower than it already was. The following month, Madame Chiang paid a visit to the United States, publicly to encourage support for China and privately to press Roosevelt and his advisors to meet her husband's demands. After the departure of the Arnold mission,

Madame Chiang Kai-shek visited the US to get support for Chiang and acceptance for her husband's demands

Chiang sent Roosevelt a letter in which he praised Chennault as a man of genius who had the complete confidence of the Chinese people. With 500 planes, an independent command, and an adequate portion of the hump tonnage, Chennault could accomplish all that he claimed.

Despite Marshall's opposition, Roosevelt quickly determined to agree, both because he was genuinely impressed with Chennault and because the news from China from all sources strongly indicated that if the American government wanted Chinese resistance to continue, it had better opt for measures designed to bring quick relief. On 8th March, the Fourteenth Air Force was created and Chennault promoted to Major General. Roosevelt told Marshall that he was 'still hopeful for the Burma operation'. but that he wanted the emphasis on Chenn-

ault's program in 1943 and that the airfield program in Assam must be pushed to the limit to provide the necessary support. While reporting to Stilwell as Theater Commander, Chennault was to have complete control over his tactics and operations, to receive 1,500 of the first 4,000 tons monthly of the airlift, and anything over 4,000 up to a total of 2,500 tons. Roosevelt also ordered that control of the hump be shifted from Bissell to Chennault but did not issue an executive order in the matter on Arnold's assurance that the transfer would be made. Although controlled operationally by ATC, what supplies were carried for whom was determined by a Tenth Air Force Board on which Chennault had no representative. To serve as chief of staff for Chennault, Arnold sent Brigadier-General Edgar Glenn who carried a written order to Stilwell for the transfer of the airlift control to the Fourteenth Air Force. The transfer was never made as Stilwell ignored the order. Chennault

General Edgar Glenn, sent by Arnold to be Chennault's chief of staff

also did not get priority in tonnage as ordered by Roosevelt because Stilwell continued to build up his Y force in Yunnan.

Chiang continued to press Roosevelt for an all-out air offensive. In April, T V Soong reported to the President: 'I am instructed by the Generalissimo that after careful consideration he has concluded all resources must be concentrated in the immediate future on launching an air offensive in China. Specifically, after weighing the various claims, he now desires that the entire air transport tonnage during the months of May, June, and July be devoted ... to building up the required reserves for decisive offensive action ...' Chiang also urged the President to call Chennault to Washington to hear his views at first hand, an idea which Roosevelt already had in mind. At Marshall's insistence, Stilwell was also summoned. Roosevelt had already decided to approve the air offensive but did not want to tell Chiang until the matter had been discussed with the British at the upcoming Trident Conference in Washington.

Held in May, the Trident Conference had as its primary purpose the determination of the time and place for the invasion of Europe while its secondary purpose was to formulate for the first time an Allied policy for the war in Asia. During the conference, the basic policy differences between the British and the Americans emerged much more sharply than at Casablanca. The British made it quite clear that they did not want to devote to China and Burma effort and resources which were urgently needed elsewhere. Churchill had an essentially political view of the war in Asia and wanted to bypass Burma in favor of Singapore, 'the only prize that will restore British prestige in this region'. Unconcerned about a possible breakdown of the war effort in China and its consequences, Chur-

Above: A Chinese soldier guards a Fourteenth Air Force bomber
Below: A bomb stockpile at the Fourteenth Air Force Headquarters in China

chill later wrote that the Americans had 'exaggerated ideas of the military power China could exert if given sufficient arms and equipment . . . and feared unduly the imminence of a Chinese collapse.'

Roosevelt by contrast was under heavy Chinese pressure for decisive action. The day before the conference opened, T V Soong told the Combined Chiefs of Staff that China would make a separate peace with Japan – an oft-used but reliable threat – unless adequate measures were taken to relieve her and carry out the promises of Casablanca. The following day Roosevelt told him that Chiang's most urgent requests would be met. The Fourteenth Air Force was to receive a substantial guaranteed tonnage and the hump tonnage was to be raised to 10,000 by September. Chennault was to have main priority but the Burma operation was kept on the schedule for November. Thus American policy was set even before the conference opened as a result of Chinese pressure and Roosevelt's own leanings.

At the conference, Stilwell and his supporters held to his original plan for a campaign in Burma as a necessary prerequisite to establishing air bases in China from which to bomb Japan. Citing Bissell's view that the hump could not be significantly expanded, Stilwell argued that the Burma operation was necessary to reopen land communications and a major supply effort for China. His case against the air offensive was that it would provoke a Japanese reaction against the Fourteenth Air Force bases in east China which Chiang's army was incapable of defending. Maintaining that the Burma offensive would be long drawn out, Chennault said that China might collapse before then. An air campaign could give the Chinese immediate succor and prepare the way for the seizure of a port on the China coast, already under consideration by Allied planners and a far better way of getting quantities of material to Chiang's forces. Raising his needs to 150 fighters, seventy medium and thirty-five heavy bombers, Chennault proposed that China could contribute to the overall Pacific strategy by creating an effective air flank for the American sweep across the Pacific. Representing the Chinese position, T V Soong spoke against Burma and in favor of developing the hump by saying that China could not wait for the Ledo Road. Unwilling to fight in Burma, the British also supported the development of the hump.

Two significant decisions concerning CBI were taken at Trident. Roosevelt agreed fully to Chennault's air offensive and again ordered him to have first priority on supplies. The Combined Chiefs of Staff abandoned ANAKIM and replaced it with a more modest operation, code named SAUCY, for the recovery only of north Burma. Utilizing only Stilwell's X and Y forces, SAUCY meant that rather than reopening the original Rangoon-Lashio-Kunming route of the Burma Road, land communications with China would run from Ledo in Assam via Myitkyina to Kunming, a route entailing almost as many logistic difficulties as the airlift itself.

Trident was a major triumph for Chennault. He presented his case persuasively and impressed both Roosevelt and the British. He was, of course, aided by the fact that he was presenting a plan already approved by Roosevelt and by the implicit opposition to Stilwell of the British who had had their share of problems with him. Obviously uncomfortable in the conference situation and displeased at being required to submit his plans to open debate, Stilwell was testy and inarticulate, a disappointment to his strong supporters Marshall and Stimson. The decision to support Chennault's plan left Stilwell in the embarrassing position of carrying out a subordinate's plan with which he had publicly and violently disagreed. Normal procedure called for his replacement and such was Roosevelt's intention until Marshall and Stimson dissuaded him with a strong defense of Stilwell.

Trident is unquestionably the key event in the history of the hump airlift. The nature of CBI was such that any course of action was totally dependent on the ability of the airlift to provide support. Up to the time of Trident, no commitment to major action had been made in CBI, hence the hump had been allowed to flounder. Once a primary commitment had been made to the air offensive and a secondary commitment to the recovery of north Burma, it went without saying that the highest immediate priority in CBI had to be the development of the airlift, without which nothing else was possible.

As a result of Trident, Roosevelt ordered the lift to reach a minimum of 7,000 tons by July and 10,000 tons by September. The Fourteenth Air Force was to get priority on 4,700 tons a month for the projected air offensive, Stilwell the next 2,000 for equipping his Yunnan forces, and the remainder to be split between the air and ground forces at Stilwell's discretion. More

General Howard Davidson. He succeeded Bissell as commander of the Tenth Air Force

men and planes were to be sent to the India-China Wing but, most crucially, a maximum effort was to be made to solve the problems in India and Assam. During the conference, Stimson discussed the Indian situation thoroughly with Churchill who said that he was not satisfied with the actions of his commanders, that he was going to change them and see that 'more punch was put into the effort'. From then on, CBI was to see the first major resources and effort committed to the airlift as a result of the Trident Conference.

After Trident, the pressure from Chiang, Chennault, and their American supporters did not ease up. Chiang asked for the replacement of Bissell who accordingly was succeeded as Commander of the Tenth Air Force by Brigadier-General Howard Davidson in July. Anticipating next a move to give Chennault control of all CBI air forces, the War Department countered by appointing Major-General

George Stratemeyer as Theater Air Commander. Instructed not to interfere with the special relations between Chennault and Chiang, Stratemeyer was given only advisory authority over the Fourteenth Air Force. In terms of air command, therefore, the theater had been in effect divided into China and India-Burma. Under Stratemeyer came the Tenth Air Force, CBI Air Service Command, supply and maintenance of the Fourteenth Air Force, protection of the hump route, coordination of theater operations with those of the India-China Wing, and assistance to Stilwell in planning air warfare. ATC remained in control of the airlift. With this move, the structure of command in CBI, already complex, became more complicated and cumbersome. It remained for the Quadrant Conference to confuse the situation further.

Held in August at Quebec, Quadrant saw all the old disputes of Trident reargued but no major departures from existing strategy were taken. Churchill maintained his view that the recapture of Burma was not necessary to defeat Japan, that this would be accomplished through sea and air action. En route to Quadrant, he had told his Chiefs of Staff, 'I remain absolutely where I was at the last conference . . . that a campaign through Rangoon up the Irrawaddy to Mandalay and beyond would be most detrimental and disadvantageous to us.' Some support for the British point of view had begun to appear in American military circles by that time. The lower level planning echelons of the War Department were arguing that the existing China strategy was defective in that China was an ineffective ally, Britain's Indian forces were incapable of mounting an offensive, the Assam line of communications was still weak, while Japan remained in a strong defensive position. Supported by a group of senior officers, the planners recommended that the present undertakings to keep China in the war be fulfilled but

General George Stratemeyer, appointed Theater Air Commander of CBI

that no further commitments be made to CBI. And at Quadrant, Admiral Chester Nimitz and a few other ranking American officers took the position that operations in CBI were purely a cover for the coming assault on the Philippines and that all plans against Japan assumed no action by the Chinese beyond containing some enemy forces. Thus at Quadrant, a growing trend in American military thinking, largely innocent of any political considerations, was questioning the value of China in the war on strategic grounds. But since American policy with regard to China was still dominated by political rather than military factors, the American views of Trident again prevailed.

Quadrant produced a move intended to bring the British and American war effort in CBI more closely together in the form of a combined Anglo-American Southeast Asia Command (SEAC) with Lord Louis Mountbatten as Supreme Commander and Stilwell as Deputy Commander. SEAC did not include India, China, or Indo-China,

nor did it have control over ATC, the air route, and the units assigned to the defense of the airlift. In addition, the Americans reserved the right to withdraw any or all Tenth Air Force units from SEAC to protect the commitments to China. An integrated command was established through the exchange of staff officers, creating an impossible situation which took lengthy negotiations at the operational level to make workable. On balance, SEAC served more to emphasize the differences between British and American aims in Asia than to create unity. SAUCY was also rescheduled for mid-February with the addition of 3,000 American commandos, and some small British amphibious operations were planned for southern Burma in the spring.

Logistics again occupied a central position in the planning for CBI at the conference. Keenly aware of the relation between logistics and victory, the conference had to recognize the fact that existing logistics simply could not move enough supplies to support both the air offensive and SAUCY. Thus an impressive list of engineering projects was devised to improve the movement of supplies in the theater, The hump tonnage was to be raised to 20,000 by June 1944. With a capacity of 30,000 tons per month, the Ledo Road was to be in operation by January 1945. A pipeline was to be constructed next to the road all the way to Kunming. With the expansion of the air route and the addition of the Ledo Road, solving the bottleneck between India and Assam became crucial to the success of the projected tactical operations in CBI. The Americans were therefore to take over the Assam-Bengal Railroad and the Brahmaputra river barge line and a six inch pipeline was to be built between Calcutta and

Generals Stratemeyer and Davidson greet the new SEAC Supreme Commander, Admiral Louis Mountbatten, on his arrival in Delhi

Chiang Kai-shek, Roosevelt, Churchill, and Madame Chiang at the Sextant Conference in Cairo

Stalin, Roosevelt, and Churchill confer with some of the Combined Chiefs of Staff at the Teheran Conference

Assam to carry gasoline for ATC planes.

Up to the Quadrant Conference, American strategy did not question the value of China's potential contribution to the war but rather how best and most quickly to realize that contribution. Quadrant is therefore significant because it revealed the extent to which American military thinking about China was shifting. Held four months later in Cairo, the Sextant Conference had a profound influence on Roosevelt and the course of Sino-American relations. To that point, Roosevelt had based his Far Eastern policy on four general ideas. First, the Chinese must reach an agreement with the Soviet Union to prevent Soviet interference after the war. Second, China must get back all of her territories, including Hong Kong. Third, Chiang's régime must be supported as the only one capable of unifying China. Fourth, American policy must be predicated on a close working relationship with China after the war. Accompanied by Stilwell, Chiang had been invited to Cairo to join in the discussions concerning CBI, so for the first time Roosevelt experienced directly the difficulties of dealing with the Chinese leader. After the conference, it was clear that his ideas about China had begun to change markedly

The conference began well enough when Chiang finally and firmly committed his Yunnan forces to the Burma campaign in return for a guarantee of British amphibious operations in the south. The United States and Britain then issued the Cairo Declaration in which they agreed to ensure the return of all territories taken from China by Japan after the war. After these initial accomplishments, Roosevelt and Churchill left to meet Stalin in Teheran. Roosevelt returned to Cairo with Stalin's promise to enter the war against Japan after the defeat of Germany and with the strong feeling that the Soviet leader could be drawn into postwar cooperation for common

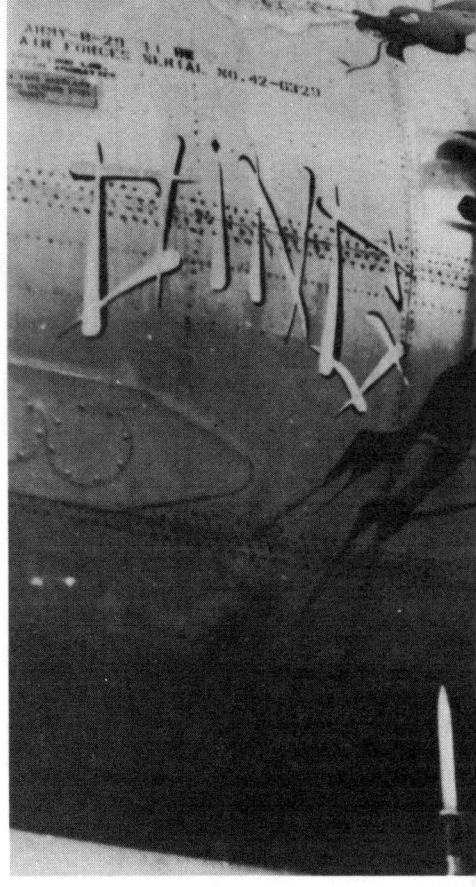

aims. In Roosevelt's eyes, these developments cast a different light on both the need for China's military contribution and the need to make China a postwar great power. On his return to Cairo, he therefore adopted a firmer attitude with Chiang, cancelling the amphibious operation and insisting that Chiang's armies must take offensive action in return for lend-lease. Predictably, Chiang resisted and demanded heavy air reinforcements and a billion dollar loan to enable China to withstand the blockade for another year. Thus began a period of desultory negotiations over the loan, which was never granted, and increasing disillusion on both sides.

Roosevelt had wanted to make Cairo a success for the Chinese but the changes in his own views and Chiang's poor showing at the conference made

him sacrifice Chiang to Stalin in the end. Cairo was thus a turning point in Sino-American relations which deteriorated steadily as the earlier illusion about Chiang and the need for China was replaced by a more realistic view of Chinese weaknesses and capabilities. Attempts to improve the Chinese army generally were abandoned by Stilwell and the War Department which now suggested that the mission of CBI should be to give air support to operations in the Pacific. American military interest in China began to center increasingly on the B-29 project and Chennault's raids on Japanese sea communications. As American operations in the Pacific met with mounting success in 1944, China was to become even more of a backwater in the war.

Even though American policy was

Guarded by a Chinese soldier, a B-29 shows a dragon symbolic of China and little camels representing trips over the hump

shifting at the end of 1943, the facade of earlier commitments was maintained for political reasons. The irony of the situation is that the hump airlift, fed by Roosevelt's earlier enthusiasm, had reached the take-off point by the end of the year. In January 1944, the India-China Wing of ATC was awarded a Presidential Citation for its achievement in delivering 13,000 tons over the hump. The United States now finally had the means to meet its new commitments and to make good Roosevelt's pledge of Trident that nothing would be left undone to relieve the siege of China.

Expansion

Some of Merrill's Marauders draw a
bead on a Japanese plane about to
attack the newly captured Myitkyina
airfield

The infancy of the hump airlift under the Tenth Air Force did not augur well for its future. The northern route over the high hump had proven far more difficult and dangerous than originally supposed while little progress had been made in solving such problems as the shortage of planes, manpower, parts, gasoline, logistics, airfields and search and rescue. ATC thus inherited a difficult situation in December 1942 but had one advantage denied the Tenth Air Force. Shortly after ATC's assumption of control, Roosevelt made the first of a series of commitments to China for higher tonnage, which in turn required that greater resources be assigned to the airlift and that a serious effort be made to solve its problems. Thus almost immediately ATC became the recipient of an influx of men and planes, an influx which increased steadily throughout 1943 as the evolving Allied strategy for CBI demanded an ever greater lift. Yet even so, ATC was no more successful with the hump

than the Tenth Air Force until Roosevelt at Trident threw the weight of presidential directive behind the build-up. After that, results were both speedy and dramatic.

During his visit to Chungking in January 1943, General Arnold ordered the number of planes on the hump run increased from sixty-two to 137 in order to meet the goal of 4,000 tons in April. This increase was to consist primarily of fifty of the big new C-46s and some additional C-87s. By March the India-China Wing had been built up to seventy-six C-47s and eleven C-87s. In late April and early May, thirty C-46s were ferried to India by TWA and Northwest Airlines pilots while by early June, sixteen of the remaining twenty C-46s assigned to the wing had either arrived or were en route. All planes were being provided with two crews, so forty-six extra crews also became available to the wing. All C-46 spare parts were being routed to India to help ensure that the new planes actually stayed in service. With this wealth of reinforcements, Colonel Alexander was able to form three new transport groups and four new airways detachments in the wing. Reinforcements notwithstanding, the wing failed badly to meet the 4,000 ton goal for April and indeed, had one of its worst months in terms of tonnage. Of the 245 tons scheduled for the Fourteenth Air Force in the first ten days of April, only forty-five tons were actually delivered, forcing Chennault to suspend all operations until the situation improved. May and June showed only slight improvement with 1,887 tons being carried in the latter month.

The reasons for the breakdown are not hard to discern. ATC policies were set in Washington but freight priorities and dispatch were controlled by the Tenth Air Force in Delhi and relations between the two agencies were not necessarily cordial at this point. ATC also had no control over the loading and unloading of freight which was handled by theater troops. There

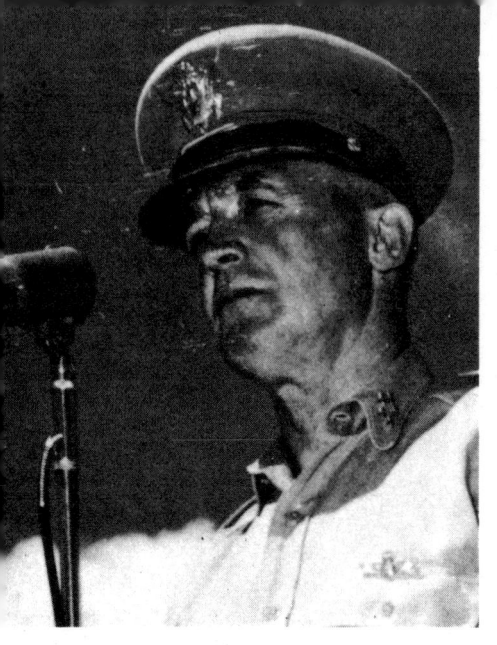

Above: General Henry Arnold, a strong supporter of the hump airlift
Below: Chabua airdrome incurred Stilwell's wrath for its filthy enlisted men's mess

were many cases of misrouting, diversion, and loss of cargo, including 'deals' whereby goods were not sent to their original destinations. The Army Services of Supply and the Air Service Command were competing for plane space and assigning their own priorities, hence all kinds of shipments were given a No 1 'must' label which slowed the entire movement of cargo since clerks could not discriminate among priorities. The command sources in India tended to give their tacit consent to these raids on cargo. Although ATC issued stern orders against the alteration of cargo priorities and addresses, the situation was not ameliorated until Stratemeyer assigned to ATC all Air Service Command and Services of Supply personnel handling ATC cargo.

There was still a severe shortage of communications, engineering, and maintenance personnel as well as radio aids and direction finders. Morale remained a major problem due to bad living conditions, outrageous

Above: 500-lb bombs at Chabua en route to the Fourteenth Air Force via the hump.
Below: Colonel Eddie Rickenbacker jokes with troops at Jorhat during his survey of the hump and its problems

The Curtiss-Wright C-46 Commando. The C-46 was derived from the CW-20 airliner project, designed before the American entry into the war. With the urgent need to supply Allied and Chinese forces in south China, the CW-20 was modified as a cargo transport aircraft, in which role it did valuable service over the hump. *Crew:* Two. *Engines:* Two Pratt & Whitney Double Wasp radials, 2,000hp each. *Speed:* 264mph: *Ceiling:* 26,000 feet. *Range:* 1,600 miles. *Weight empty/loaded:* 27,664/45,000lbs. *Span:* 108 feet. *Length:* 76 feet 4 inches

General Raymond Wheeler. He was assigned to clear up the logistic mess in India and Assam

General Earl Hoag became commander of the India-China Wing in September 1943

mail service, slow promotions, and poor messing facilities. A particularly notorious case in this last regard was the Polo Grounds Mess at ATC's Chabua airdrome where the bad conditions were tolerated by the senior base officers who could eat elsewhere. In February Stillwell arrived unannounced and sat at the filthy benches to share the messline 'slop' with the enlisted men. He then summoned the base commander and told him to have the situation remedied immediately or be relieved. Flight crews in particular had morale problems because of the unreliability of the C-46 and because they disliked risking their lives to carry what they considered unessential supplies such as brooms and filing cabinets or goods which they were reasonably certain would end up in some Chinese official's private *godown* (warehouse). On the other hand, these same crews were ready to risk anything when carrying supplies destined for the Fourteenth Air Force.

It was, however, very clear to observers that the primary factor in the failure of the hump was the sagging airdrome construction program. In April, Arnold sent Colonel Edward Rickenbacker to India specifically to

get his expert opinion on the problems of the hump. While citing all the other usual reasons, Rickenbacker's report emphasized the lack of airdrome facilities as the key factor. At the same time, Alexander saw the mission of his India-China Wing seriously threatened by the failure of the British to complete the complex of bases in Assam and wrote to Arnold that 'in view of the potential political repercussions which may result from non-delivery of supplies to China and possible annoyance and embarrassment to you, [representations must be made] to Mr Churchill, if necessary, to build a fire under General Wavell and get some action on ATC airdromes in Assam.'

The situation was without question as grave as reported. In the spring of 1943 the monsoon arrived a month early, forcing all air traffic to use only the two all-weather fields at Dinjan and Chabua. With Dinjan occupied by CNAC and the 51st Fighter Group, ATC now shared Chabua with the 308th Heavy Bomber Group under impossibly crowded conditions. Fifty C-47s, C-87s and B-24s had to be parked in rows in daylight with an estimated 277 enemy planes based only three hours away in Burma. Thus by the time of Trident, it was quite clear to all parties where the major effort had to be made.

With the weight of Roosevelt and Churchill behind it, an order was issued by the Combined Chiefs of Staff on 22nd May that Chabua, Mohanbari, Sookerating, and Jorhat, in that order of priority, were to be completed by 1st July with a minimum of twenty hardstandings each. Steel landing mat was to be used if necessary to meet the goal of 7,000 tons in July and 10,000 in September. Major General Raymond Wheeler, chief of the Army Services of Supply in CBI, was charged with responsibility for the airdrome program and ordered to complete a minimum of seven airdromes with 6,000 foot runways and forty hardstandings each by September. Wheeler was told to ask Marshall directly for any help he needed in extracting the basics for the airdrome program from General Headquarters in India and to make weekly progress reports to Marshall. Having received a strong message of its own from London, General Headquarters was now more than willing to cooperate.

With sufficient motivation from above, the combined British and American resources brought swift results. Wheeler threw all possible American resources into the program, including the construction units assigned to the Ledo Road project on which work was just beginning. Airdrome construction was removed from the control of local British commands such as the Fourth Corps and the Eastern Army Command and brought directly under General Headquarters. Wheeler assumed an active supervisory role and used American personnel and equipment to support the British rather than taking complete charge of the program – a move which he felt would have caused the

Bombs for the Fourteenth Air Force arrive in China encrusted with mud from the Indian monsoon

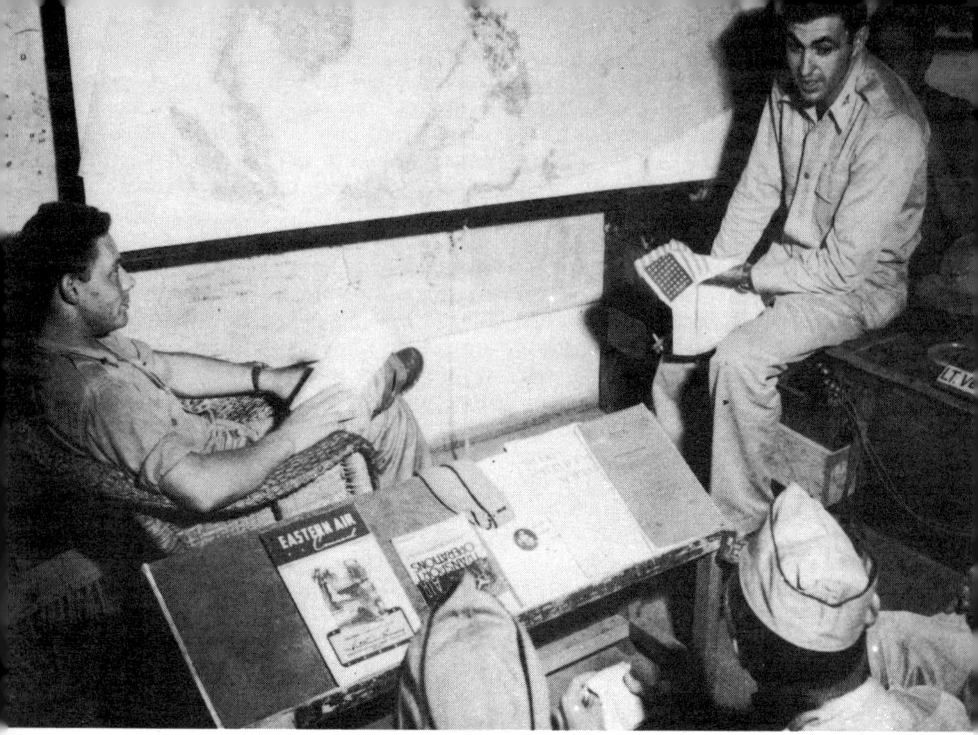

Above: New American flight crews are intensively briefed on the dangers of the hump run. *Below:* Chinese troops trained in India move down a road near Myitkyina to join their brigade

British to withdraw and thus made completion impossible. Experienced engineers were brought in and given a free hand and full powers over transport, material, and labor. Trucks, crushers, and rollers were rushed from the United States to India. The requisition of tea garden acreage was made easier, thus enabling the engineers to improve the design of the airfields.

Despite these efforts, however, Wheeler had to report to Marshall on 1st July that a total of only sixty hardstandings had been completed because of the time required to transfer units and equipment, coordinate with the British, originate new procedures, and get supplies to Assam on the creaky Assam-Bengal Railroad. But the program was moving swiftly and in August the initial four airdromes had been completed to specifications with work already under way on three new fields. Although far short of ideal, the crash program was successful enough to relegate airdrome facilities to a secondary place among ATC's problems.

While the Army Services of Supply was racing to complete the airdrome program, ATC was preparing to meet the new tonnage quotas with a buildup of personnel and planes. In June ATC launched Project 7, its largest overseas movement of men and planes to date, to bring additional reinforcements to the India-China Wing. This was followed by Project 7a in July, a four-month contract with American Airlines to provide twenty-five flight crews and maintenance personnel to fly C-87s from the new ATC base at Tezpur. Operating with seven to ten planes, Project 7a delivered 2,500 tons, mostly gasoline and bombs for the Fourteenth Air Force. The lift received unexpected assistance from Project 8 as well. Intended to fly material for the proposed Assam-China pipeline, the sixteen C-47s and forty C-46s assigned to the project were to join the airlift temporarily until the pipeline supplies arrived. The material

never did appear, so the planes of Project 8 became a *de facto* part of the regular hump operations. ATC thus increased the personnel and planes of its India-China Wing from 2,759 men and 108 planes in June to 10,851 men and 249 planes in December.

The India-China Wing came under new management in September. Alexander was replaced as commander by Brigadier-General Earl Hoag and Colonel Thomas Hardin was transferred from ATC's Central Africa Sector to take direct charge of the hump operations. A hard-driving former airlines executive, Hardin immediately set out to whip the airlift into shape. One of his first general orders decreed, 'Effective immediately, there will be no more weather over the hump', which meant that pilots were to take a bolder attitude toward the weather and were not to cancel flights because of storms. Another order forbade cancelling flights because of reports of enemy planes. As a result, six transports were shot down on 13th October but a new one-day record of 200 tons went over the hump. Five more planes were lost on 23rd October but another new record of 300 tons was set. That same month, Hardin introduced night flights on the hump run, stating that 'crews have to sleep but the planes don't'. In this way, he was able to double the possible utilization of the available planes, especially important at that time because a high number of transports were grounded daily. In August, for example, a daily average of 100 ATC planes were out of service, mostly for maintenance reasons. Hardin also made a determined effort to secure control of the China terminals used by ATC but his attempts were defeated by Chennault.

Although the Operations Planning Division of the War Department concluded that a maximum effort had been made to increase the hump tonnage in the summer of 1943, ATC once again failed to meet the goals set for it. From a lowly 1,887 tons in June, the lift grew to 3,451 in July and 4,624 in September, a far cry from the 7,000 and 10,000 ton quotas ordered by Roosevelt at Trident. ATC defended itself by arguing that it was still trying to overcome the legacy of the Tenth Air Force and that supporting units and equipment not under ATC control were still regularly given assignments unrelated to the airlift. In Washington, the situation was seen as serious. Roosevelt wrote to Marshall that he

Tanks destined for the Burma and China fronts are temporarily stored along Hospital Road in Calcutta

was disgusted with 'the India-China matter. Everything seems to go wrong. But the worst thing is that we are falling down on our promises every time.' But the progress with the airdrome program, the increase in men and planes, and Hardin's vigorous management all combined to effect a steady increase in the lift. The October tonnage was up to 7,000, the November tonnage to 9,436 while in December, the 10,000-ton goal was finally reached with a lift of 12,590, a feat for which the India-China Wing received a Presidential Citation.

The achievement of the 10,000-ton

lift was not without its cost, however, as the pressure took a grave toll of men and planes. Between June and December 1943, the hump route suffered 135 major accidents with a total of 168 crew fatalities. After the introduction of night flying in October, there were thirty-eight major accidents over the hump in November and twenty-eight in December. It was at this point that the wing really began to develop extensive search and rescue operations. The inexperience of flight crews was a key factor in the increasing incidence of accidents as General Hoag reported to Arnold:

'With the experience level here, we are going to pay dearly for the tonnage moved across the hump.' A program to upgrade the training of flight crews was instituted but accidents remained a serious problem on the hump run until the end of hostilities in August 1945, after which ATC stressed safety over tonnage.

The achievement of the 10,000-ton lift also led Hoag, Hardin, and Stratemeyer to worry about orders for further increases. As the war wound up to its climax in CBI, they had to face the question of how to raise the hump tonnage higher or see some other agency move in. In the words of an ATC report, 'The pressure for additional supplies in China is actually only just beginning and we must constructively plan to expand faster than we have been called upon to undertake to date or else fall behind the war procession in the near future.' Therefore Stratemeyer appointed a board of officers to study what action might be taken by ATC and the other CBI agencies. The board arrived at two rather obvious conclusions, that substantial gains could be made through more efficient use of existing resources and by adding to those resources. Thus another augmentation plan was developed which called for three new airdromes in east Bengal, delivery of aircraft on schedule to ATC, service and repair units for the expanded hump fleet, and an airfield and gasoline supplies in the Myitkyina area, newly captured by Stilwell's Chinese forces. The plan was accepted by the War Department and although the conditions were not met on schedule, the tonnage, after holding around 13,000-14,000 tons per month from January to May 1944, took another substantial jump to 18,000 in June and 23,675 in August.

By the fall of 1943, it had become apparent that a serious effort had to be made to improve the line of communications between Calcutta and Assam. When the lift was barely a few thousand tons per month, the line of communications was no more pressing than ATC's other problems because there was always a backlog of supplies in Assam waiting to be airlifted. With the expansion of the lift due to the airdrome program and increased planes, however, the ability of ATC to fly supplies to China began rapidly to exceed the ability of the line of communications to transport the supplies to Assam. This problem had received some consideration from CBI planners at the Quadrant Conference in August 1943 and had become acute by October-November.

In the summer of 1943, the emphasis was shifting from Karachi to Calcutta as the American port of entry because the Japanese ability to menace eastern India had been reduced to occasional submarine harassment of shipping and sporadic air raids. Calcutta was only 600 miles from the main ATC

Once opened, the port of Calcutta quickly became jammed with Allied shipping

bases in Assam and even closer to the new ATC bases being built in east Bengal. The port of Calcutta was under civilian management and, under the weight of the new military traffic, completely broke down in the fall.

Whether debarked at Karachi or Calcutta, all supplies had to use the Assam-Bengal Railroad for the last leg of the journey to Assam. Rail shipment from Calcutta to Tezgaon in Bengal required ten to fifteen days while to Chabua or Jorhat required eighteen to twenty. At this time, the railroad had to support not only ATC, the Tenth Air Force, the RAF and the airdromes in Assam and Bengal but also the Chinese troops at Ramgarh, the Ledo Road project and accompanying pipeline, and the British forces in Assam, Manipur, and Arakan. As the demands on the railroad grew, the supply situation in north-east India became acute to the point that some of the British troops in Manipur and Arakan were reported to be suffering from malnutrition. Like the port,

the railroad was in civilian hands and was generally considered to suffer from lethargic and inefficient management.

No less than their American allies, the British military was a victim of this situation, hence both were agreed that the entire line of communications should be under military control. As General William Covell of the Army Services of Supply wrote to Marshall: '. . . our biggest headache has been with the line of communications from Calcutta to Assam which is in British civilian hands. We get all kinds of promises but nothing happens. As a result, for the last two weeks, I have been raising hell but still feel that more drastic action may be necessary.' Covell and his British colleagues then learned that their proposal for military control had been blocked by the War Transport Department of the Indian Government which wanted the port to remain under the control of a commissioner prominently identified with the exist-

ing colonial régime. At this point, Marshall felt that 'more drastic action' was indeed called for and told Roosevelt that the situation in India was 'precarious,' that three of the ATC fields in which he took such an interest were literally out of gas, that military control was the only solution, and that Churchill must be so informed. Roosevelt in turn wrote to Churchill that the operations of ATC were being embarrassed by a lack of vigorous management on the Assam line of communications and asked him to intervene personally. Although Churchill promised an investigation, the issue had already been decided in favor of the military by Governor-General Wavell in India. Perhaps remembering how his own operations in Burma in 1942 had been hobbled by logistic problems, Wavell personally ordered that a complete change-over be made, making his wishes known to the civilian opponents of military control 'with the accompaniment of a little desk pounding'.

Indian laborers handle gasoline drums at one of the Assam bases in monsoon weather

The Anglo-American military moved quickly to take over in January 1944. At Calcutta, a British port commissioner with an American assistant divided the dock area into British and American sections and organized the pooling of dock labor and lighters. In its section of the port, the Services of Supply put ten companies of port troops to work clearing the congestion, introduced a twenty-four hour working day and more equipment, and replaced native labor wherever possible with American troops. By April Covell was able to report '. . . no special concern need be given to the capacity of the port of Calcutta, nor has any indication been given at this time that it has reached its saturation point'.

The Assam-Bengal Railroad presented not only engineering problems but a conflict in management philosophy as well. A broad gauge line ran north-east from Calcutta but changed to a metre gauge line halfway to Assam. The broad gauge line could carry more freight than the metre

gauge could receive and neither was double-tracked. The transshipment points and the ferries over the Brahmaputra river, however, were considered the major bottlenecks on the line. The Indian Government had plans for a bridge, double-tracking the whole line, and new yards but, to the despair of the military, only 3·25 miles of track were laid between July 1943 and April 1944. In terms of management, the civilian administration determined the capacity of the line, set that as a target, and then refused to exceed it. The civilian management also believed that the flow of loaded cars going to Assam must be balanced by a return flow of empty cars as opposed to the military which saw the movement of freight as primary rather than the balance of rolling stock.

A quick American survey concluded that the railroad's greatest deficiency was lack of 'aggressive adequate supervisory staff between management and actual operating personnel'. Rather than trying to rebuild the line, more efficient and vigorous operating methods would bring a sharp and immediate increase in tonnage. Thus in January 1944 the Anglo-American

Above: Chinese troops training in India march along the Assam-Bengal Railroad to a rail depot. *Below:* The enormous quantities of gasoline used on the hump run could be loaded in any one of several ways at the Assam bases

Military Railway Service was formed and seven battalions of American railroad troops were superimposed on the existing railroad staff to operate key sections of the line. The ferries were operated efficiently, train speeds were increased, train lengths doubled, and all unnecessary stops and delays were eliminated. While February

These P-40s were part of the defense of the Assam bases against Japanese attack

showed some increase in the line's capacity, March brought a 44·6 per cent jump in tonnage. After March the railroad ceased to be a problem despite the additional strain imposed by the Japanese invasion of Assam. The Military Railway Service moved all traffic required of it and also handled sixty-four troop trains between 23rd March and 18th April, an indication of the swift change in the line's condition. In June all cargo requests were accepted 'as is', while in

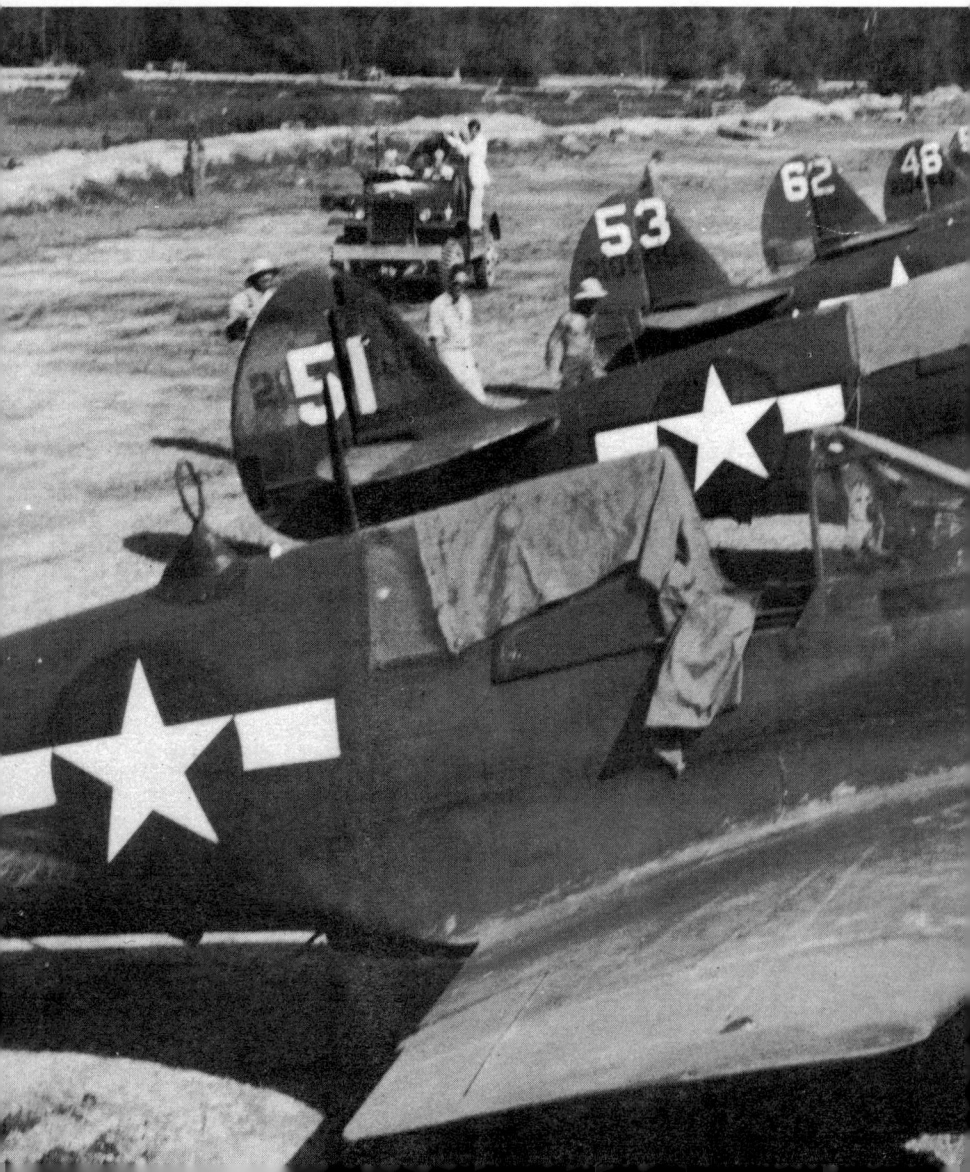

July the Military Railway Service reported that it had surplus capacity. Had the railroad not undergone this change in management, it is doubtful whether north-east India could have been supported logistically to resist the March invasion of the Japanese.

Gasoline constituted a special supply problem since ATC alone used enormous quantities on the hump run. Until mid-1944 air operations were generally limited by fuel shortages. The Quadrant planners had deter-mined to build up the barge traffic on the Brahmaputra river and to lay pipelines between Calcutta and Assam. Some equipment was sent for the barge line but it was not very successful, hence most of it was assigned ultimately to the ferries and the Calcutta harbor instead. In November 1944, construction began on six-inch and four-inch lines from the port of Chittagong to the new ATC base at Tinsukia. Another six-inch line was built from Calcutta to Tinsukia and

to a second new ATC base at Kharagpur. Since no special engineering problems were involved, construction moved quickly and gasoline supplies improved to the point where they were considered adequate at seven of ATC's nine bases. To illustrate the magnitude of the problem, ATC was consuming 400,000 imperial gallons of gasoline per day in October 1944, 700,000 imperial gallons in May 1945, and 900,000 imperial or 1,080,865 American gallons in July 1945.

Among the factors controlling the expansion of the airlift in 1943-1944 were the counter-operations of the Japanese air force in Burma. With 277 planes in Burma, well equipped bases in rear areas, many forward airstrips, and experienced pilots, the Japanese were a formidable foe in the air. After the attacks on Assam in October 1942, the Allies had only forty P-40 fighters to defend Assam and patrol the hump

Tenth Air Force B-25s bomb a Japanese base at Myebon, Burma, during the struggle for air superiority

route. As 1943 progressed, however, more fighter squadrons with newer model planes were assigned to CBI, thus enabling the Allies to fight off Japanese raids on Assam and the hump and launch sustained air operations over Burma. Throughout 1943 and the first half of 1944, the Tenth Air Force and the RAF waged a vigorous struggle with the enemy for air superiority over Burma.

In February 1943, forty-two enemy planes raided Dinjan but suffered heavy losses. In May, thirty-five planes bombed Calcutta, causing light damage but still demonstrating the Japanese ability to strike at India's largest city. The fall again brought a large scale attempt to harass the hump. For a period of several weeks in October, enemy fighter sweeps, aided by ground radio reports, bagged two or three transports per day over the hump. This particular episode ended when a formation of freight hauling B-24s belonging to the Fourteenth Air Force, evidently mistaken for unarmed C-87s, inflicted heavy

losses on its attackers. December saw new raids on the hump and several attacks on the China terminals. January of 1944 brought a last spectacular attempt to dominate the hump route by the Japanese who sent out sweeps of up to fifty planes for eight consecutive days. Tenth Air Force and RAF planes successfully met this attack and again forced the Japanese to withdraw.

Toward the end of 1943, the initiative in the air was passing to the Allies. Now at the head of the newly-formed Anglo-American Eastern Air Command, Stratemeyer was in a position to challenge the Japanese once and for all for air superiority over Burma. With combined AAF and RAF forces of 576 fighters, seventy medium bombers, and seventy-nine heavy bombers, he launched a series of moderately successful attacks on Japanese installations in southern Burma. These stimulated the enemy to move in reinforcements, however, and did not in the end diminish his strength. The issue was finally decided in March when the Japanese threw the bulk of their planes into support of the Assam invasion. The Third Tactical Air Force under Air Marshal Sir John Baldwin, a unit of the Eastern Air Command, broke the back of the Japanese air force in Burma by destroying 117 of its planes which forced it into essentially defensive actions. By May, eighty-five more Japanese planes had been destroyed and Allied control of the air over Burma could no longer be challenged. The 100 fighters assigned solely to the defense of the hump were released for other duty. Combined with Stilwell's capture of the Myitkyina airfield in the same month, the defeat of the Japanese air force meant that the airlift was now totally free of enemy harassment and able once again to use the more southerly, lower route over the hump. These two events were key factors in freeing the airlift for the almost untrammeled expansion of hump tonnage which began in the summer of 1944.

From June 1943 to June 1944, air-

Above: A C-47 bound for China takes off from Myitkyina after the airfield was recaptured in May 1944. *Below:* Chinese reinforcements arrive as soon as the Myitkyina airfield is secured

Above: American commandos fought alongside Chinese troops in north Burma
Below: British Chindits, some wounded, await air evacuation from the central Burma jungle

Brigadier Orde Wingate of the Chindits

drome facilities in Assam were tripled, the number of transports on the hump run was tripled, repair and maintenance efficiency was doubled, and with the introduction of the twenty-four hour schedule, the possible number of flights was doubled. As a result, tonnage went from 1,887 to 18,235, a tenfold increase. It is likely that an even higher growth could have been achieved in the first half of 1944 and thereafter had it not been for the fact that both the Allies and the Japanese undertook major offensive action in CBI during the winter of 1944. Stilwell launched his north Burma drive, Wingate's Chindits began operations in central Burma while the Japanese mounted major drives against Assam and then east China. In all cases, whether offensive or defensive, new strains were placed on the hump as the Allies called on the air transport services available to make large scale troop movements within the theater or to supply the forces in Burma. Although the main burden was not always on ATC, which shared it with the Troop Carrier Command, many diversions of transports from the regular hump operations to other duties were necessary. By this time, however, the airlift had solved its problems to a point where it was able to maintain a growing lift to China despite these diversions.

In February 1944, the Joint Chiefs of Staff adopted a Pacific strategy which embodied the growing American doubts, expressed at Quadrant and Cairo, about China's strategic value in the war. The approach to Japan was to be a two-pronged sea and air attack from the central and south Pacific. As Marshall instructed Stilwell, the 'paramount mission in the China Theater' was now to 'support the main effort directed against the enemy by forces in the Pacific.' Stilwell was now to devote his chief effort 'to the hump lift and its security'. The Fourteenth Air Force was to be built up and 5,000 tons a month were to be stocked in China to support Chennault's reinforced air force when the time came to support the Allied attack on Luzon or Formosa. To aid the airlift, Stilwell was to clear upper Burma while Mountbatten's SEAC forces were to seize Rangoon to help force an enemy evacuation of upper Burma. The recapture of upper Burma was to have a major impact on the airlift.

That same month, the long-discussed Allied offensives in Burma were launched. Stilwell's X force pushed into the Hukawng Valley from Ledo and, after some coaxing, the Y force began a cautious advance from Yunnan. At the same time, the 22,000 troops of the Indian 5th and 7th Divisions were surrounded by the enemy in Arakan and, supplied by air, had to fight their way out under the leadership of General William Slim. On 5th March, 4,000 British jungle

Above: Troops of the British Fourteenth Army move down the Imphal-Kohima road after the Japanese invasion of Assam has been turned back
Below: Kachin tribesmen and some of Merrill's Maurauders watch a supply drop in north Burma

Above: Air supply made possible the Allied successes at Imphal and in north Burma
Below: Chinese troops at Yunnanyi await airlift to the Salween front in Burma

troops known as Chindits and led by Brigadier Orde Wingate began a deep penetration behind Japanese lines in Burma, entirely dependent on air supply. On 8th March, to the great surprise of the Allies who had expected an attack by several regiments, 155,000 Japanese troops began a strong drive against Assam, the last full-scale enemy offensive in Burma. Japanese goals were to occupy Indian soil for political reasons, capture the big British base at Imphal, and cut the Assam-Bengal Railroad in the Kohima-Dimapur area. Had the Japanese offensive been successful, it would not only have struck a fatal blow to British rule in India but would have cut off Stilwell's forces in north Burma and completed the isolation of China by capturing the Indian terminals of the airlift.

By the end of the month, Imphal and Kohima were surrounded and Japanese troops were within thirty miles of the railroad. With the Third Tactical Air Force sweeping the skies of enemy planes, the Troop Carrier Command, augmented by thirty-five transports borrowed from ATC, flew in 20,125 tons of supplies and 12,622 reinforcements and airlifted out 29,710 nonessential personnel and 10,265 casualties. For three months, air supply maintained 28,000 British and 30,000 Indian troops at Imphal, supplied Wingate's Chindits in central Burma, and supplied much of Stilwell's needs as well while maintaining an average of 14,000 tons per month over the hump. The brunt of the air supply operations was borne by the Troop Carrier Command but ATC had to divert a substantial number of its planes to assist in the direct defense of the region. Hardin, by then a general and commander of the India-China Wing, estimated that these diversions cost the hump deliveries a total of 2,500 tons.

In April, ATC was called upon to transport the 18,000 troops of the Chinese 50th Division from Yunnan to Sookerating whence Troop Carrier planes and ground transport moved them into Burma as badly needed reinforcements for Stilwell. Hardin believed that this movement reduced the airlift by 1,500 tons and so reported to ATC headquarters in Washington where the tonnage figure had become almost a fetish and the sole measure of the Wing's accomplishment.

ATC soon had another chore to perform for Stilwell but this time the assignment was most welcome. On 17th May Stilwell's forces captured the Myitkyina airfield, although the town itself did not fall until August. On 18th May ATC planes flew in 2,500 combat troops and 250 airborne engineers, their bulldozers, tractors, and other equipment. The capture of Myitkyina removed the main base from which the Japanese had harassed the hump, made it possible for ATC planes to use again the southern route over the hump, and later provided an important transit base for the hump flights. More than any other factor, the conquest of north Burma was responsible for the startling jumps in the hump tonnage which occurred after June. Thus while Chennault criticized the expenditure of air supply on Stilwell's campaign, Hardin and the ATC headquarters in Washington generally favored it because it had a direct bearing on the India-China Wing's primary mission, the relief of China.

The end of enemy air harassment and the reopening of the southern hump route could not have come at a more opportune moment for the airlift because in April, the Japanese, long quiescent, broke the military stalemate in China by launching their largest land offensive of the war, an offensive which ultimately involved 620,000 of their troops. Code named 'Ichigo', its goals were to 'forestall the bombing of the homeland by American B-29s based at Kweilin and Liuchow' and to 'destroy the backbone of the Chinese army and force increased deterioration of the political régime.' The Japanese intended to establish a corridor between Man-

Chinese civilians evacuate Kweilin before advancing Japanese troops in 1944

Chungking on the Yangtze river was the war-time capital of China

churia-north China and French Indo-China and to eliminate the Fourteenth Air Force bases in east China. If Ichigo was successful, the Japanese planned to drive up the Yangtze valley on Chungking, whose fall would have decisively taken China out of the war.

The Chinese armies were incapable of stopping the offensive since the best units and the bulk of lend-lease was in Burma. The Fourteenth Air Force, often castigated for its failure to halt the offensive, was in actuality in desperate straits. Three squadrons were supporting the Burma campaign while the entire 312th Fighter Wing was tied to the defense of the four B-29 bases at Chengtu by specific order of the War Department. More than planes, however, a shortage of fuel constituted the critical factor. The supply quota of the Fourteenth Air Force had been reduced due to the stockpiling for the B-29 project, hence fuel reserves were generally low and acutely low at the threatened east

China bases. The shortage could not be quickly eliminated because it took a month for supplies to reach east China from Kunming or the other hump terminals in west China. Chennault appealed to Stilwell for additional hump tonnage. which Stilwell gave him, and for permission to use the B-29 stockpiles, which Marshall and Arnold refused. The effect of the additional hump supplies was not felt until August when the battle for the airfields was in its last stage. By October. all the airfields had been lost and the Manchuria-Hanoi corridor was completed. Ichigo had achieved its immediate goals. east China was isolated. Chiang's political prestige had received a disastrous blow, and the road to Chungking apparently lay open to the enemy.

The Ichigo crisis placed a special strain on the India-China Division (all ATC wings were raised to division status on 1st July 1944) whose mission was to carry aid to China and thus found its very reason for existence at stake. The emergency intensified the urgency of increasing tonnage to the maximum but also called on the Division to perform special missions.

Between 1st April and 11th May, the entire Chinese Sixth Army was airlifted from Chanyi, Chenkung, Luliang, and Kunming to assist in the defense of Chihkiang. 1,648 trips were required to move 25,136 troops, 2,178 horses, and 1,565 tons of equipment. Code named ROOSTER, the movement enabled the Chinese to beat back the Japanese with heavy losses and secure the base. ATC planes also flew supplies to the various bases under attack and then helped to evacuate them as they fell one by one. Without the assistance of ATC, the Chinese defense of east China would have collapsed far more quickly and enabled the Japanese to open their Yangtze drive before preparations for its defense were complete.

The debacle caused by Ichigo brought on another major crisis in Sino-American relations. In refusing to give Chennault the B-29 supplies, Marshall had concluded that the immense effort to supply Chennault had been a 'poorly directed and possibly completely wasteful procedure' as he wrote to Roosevelt. Stimson also was bitter about the fact that the diversion of so many transports to the hump was likely 'to cost us an extra winter in the main theater of war'. Disgusted with the situation, the Joint Chiefs of Staff seriously considered ending support to China and abandoning the airlift but finally decided that such a course of action would greatly strengthen the Japanese will to fight. In the belief that the only hope of salvaging the situation in China lay in giving Stilwell complete command of all Chinese forces, Marshall broached this idea to Roosevelt who by this time was also disillusioned and now ready to try Stilwell as he had once tried Chennault. The proposal to make Stilwell commander of all Chinese forces, however, was rejected by Chiang who in addition demanded Stilwell's recall, to which Roosevelt finally agreed. Thus, in October, Major-General Albert Wedemeyer replaced Stilwell in the China Theater which was separated from the India-Burma Theater.

As a result of this episode, Sino-

An unwilling mule is loaded aboard a transport during Operation Rooster

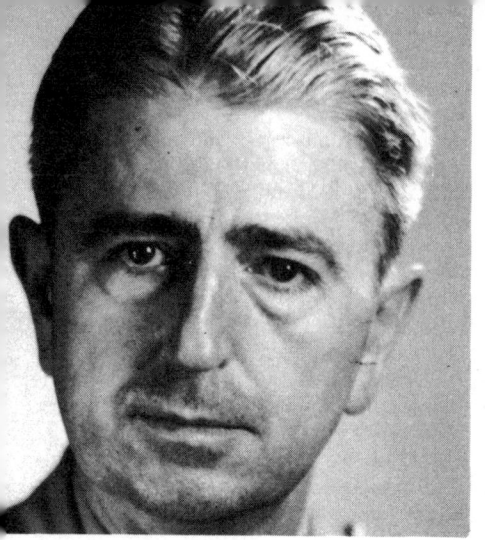

General Albert Wedemeyer succeeded Stilwell as commander of US forces in China

American political relations reached a new low but the military situation in China began to improve. A completely different personality from Stilwell, Wedemeyer proved able to work with the Chinese and made progress in training and equipping Chinese divisions around Chungking. Foreseeing that the next Japanese blow would be struck against western China, Chiang and Wedemeyer requested that most of the Chinese troops in Burma be returned to China. Under the direction of the Tenth Air Force, Operation Grubworm was accordingly planned to move the Chinese 14th and 22nd Divisions, a total of 25,095 troops. Grubworm had to be accomplished with the minimum possible interference with the two other major transport obligations in CBI, the hump airlift which delivered 31,935 tons in December 1944, the same month as Grubworm, and the air supply of the Burma campaign. At this time, seven British divisions, three Chinese divisions, three infantry brigades, and two tank brigades (around 300,000 troops) were receiving ninety per cent of their supplies by air in Burma. Thus any new transport

obligation was a serious undertaking. Two Tenth Air Force Troop Carrier squadrons and two ATC squadrons with additional transports borrowed from air commando units flew a twenty-four hour per day schedule. The 1348th ATC Base Unit was sent to Myitkyina to set up the operational and coordinating center for Grubworm. The 14th Division was assigned to C-46s based in Assam and Luliang while the 22nd was handled by China-based C-47s. To maintain continuous operations, crews were changed at the end of each round trip.

The Grubworm soldiers became the nucleus of a larger force being organized by Wedemeyer to counter the expected renewal of the Japanese offensive. In April 1945, the Japanese did renew their attack on Chihkiang which controlled the approaches to Chungking and Kunming. By mid-May the American trained and equipped Chinese troops had decisively defeated the Japanese and caused the beginning of a general enemy with-

Chinese soldiers hitch a ride on a US tank in Burma

drawal. Grubworm was one of the major transport achievements in CBI, a theater famous for such feats. ATC planes flew 597 sorties and Tenth Air Force planes 731 sorties with the loss of only three planes.

Concurrent with the supply of the Burma campaign, the regular hump operations, and the crisis caused by Ichigo, ATC had a further burden imposed on it during 1944 in the form of Project MATTERHORN which brought the new and untried American super-bomber – the B-29 – to CBI. American policy had always been to use Chinese bases to bomb Japan and this American fixation unwisely wished a voracious new consumer of supplies on a theater which was already a logistic nightmare. Although most Americans in CBI had reservations about MATTERHORN, the cancelling of the amphibious operations demanded by Chiang as the price of his participation in the Burma campaign ensured that the bombers would be assigned to China as a salve for his feelings and,

in the words of Roosevelt, as a 'spur to China's war effort'. Once again, political expediency had won out over military common sense in CBI.

In February 1944, ATC was ordered to deliver a minimum of 1,650 tons and hopefully 2,275 tons to the B-29 bases at Chengtu. In March MATTERHORN received three eighths of the tonnage for the month or 3,602 tons. ATC had to assign twenty C-87s specifically to this chore. By the end of the year, approximately 30,000 tons had been flown over the hump for the B-29s in addition to what the B-29s carried for themselves. A further 4,375 tons was absorbed by the 312th Fighter Wing which had as its sole responsibility the defense of the four B-29 bases around Chengtu.

Yet all told, the B-29s flew only twenty missions from Chengtu – nine to Japan, ten to Manchuria, and one to Formosa. In the words of the

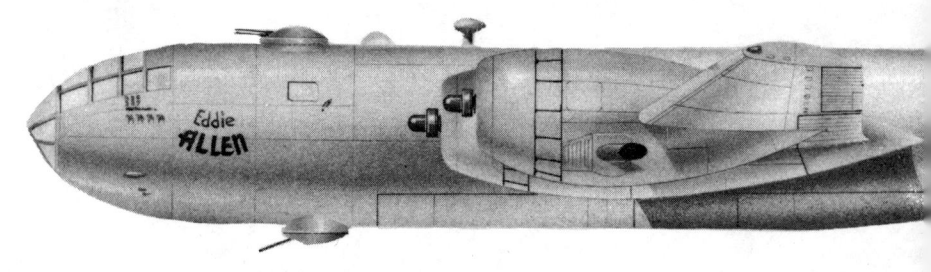

The Boeing B-29. The most sophisticated bomber produced by the US in the Second World War, the B-29 was used only in the Far East, against the Japanese. The design paid particular importance to the elimination of drag, in order to produce a good performance at altitude. To this end, the normal type of gun turret was eliminated and replaced by a low-drag remotely controlled one, the fuselage was circular and the skin was flush rivetted. The particular aircraft illustrated here was named 'Eddie Allen' after the Boeing test pilot who first flew the B-29 and later lost his life testing a subsequent B-29 prototype. The machine was on the establishment of the 45th Bombardment Squadron, part of the 40th Bombardment Group of the United States Twentieth Air Force. 'Eddie Allen' made ten trips over the hump in the transport role while serving in the Burma-China area, before going to Tinian, from which it made 23 bombing sorties. *Engines:* Four Wright R-3350 radials, 2,200hp each at takeoff. *Crew:* 11. *Speed:* 358mph at 25,000 feet. *Climb:* 38 minutes to 20,000 feet. *Ceiling:* 31,850 feet. *Range:* 3,250 miles with maximum load and 5,600 miles maximum. *Armament:* Up to 20,000lbs of bombs plus 12 .5-inch machine guns with with 11,500 rounds and one 20mm cannon with 100 rounds. *Weight empty/loaded:* 70,140/124,000lbs. *Span:* 141 feet 3 inches. *Length:* 99 feet

American-trained Chinese troops mortar Japanese forces near Chihkiang

United States Strategic Bombing Survey, these missions 'did little to hasten the Japanese surrender or justify the lavish expenditures poured out on their behalf through a fantastically uneconomic and barely workable supply system.' Because the B-29s consumed so many supplies in a theater of scarcity while contributing nothing to the theater, Wedemeyer finally prevailed on the Joint Chiefs of Staff to withdraw the bombers in January 1945. They had few mourners in China as they had been an unwarranted drain on the operations in Burma, on the Fourteenth Air Force, and on the Chinese economy, and thus had become a new source of friction in the already troubled waters of Sino-American relations.

Until mid-1943 the airlift had floundered, unable to deal effectively with its basic problems. After Trident, a determined effort was made to increase the lift in the face of the anticipated campaigns in CBI. By the summer of 1944, the airlift was delivering over twice as much as the 10,000-ton goal set for it at Trident in spite of the considerable diversions from regular hump operations caused by the Imphal crisis, air supply of the entire Burma campaign, troop movements to China, and MATTERHORN. Having passed through its infancy and adolescence, the airlift was now to enter adulthood or, as it was known in the India-China Division, the 'age of big business'.

On 7th December 1944, Chengtu-based B-29s struck the big Japanese aircraft factory at Mukden, Manchuria

Big business

Chinese troops move toward waiting
planes on a Burma airfield during
Operation Grubworm

In September 1944, after two years of arduous service in Africa and CBI. General Hardin was replaced as commander of the India-China Division by Brigadier-General William Tunner of ATC's Ferrying Division. Building on the foundation laid by Hardin, who had forced tonnage from 4,624 in September 1943 to 23,675 in August 1944, Tunner and several key officers from his ATC staff introduced some techniques of big business enterprises into the airlift, hence the men in the India-China Division called it the 'age of big business'. As tonnage increased during the fall of 1944 and the winter of 1945, there was less and less talk about a maximum figure. Tunner and his staff propounded the thesis that any tonnage could be delivered over the hump if the requisite facilities and men were provided. The constant pressure on the India-China Division for more lift brought a counter pressure from Tunner for more airfields, more planes and personnel, and improved navigational aids. At the same time, he drove for more 'production', meaning increased efficiency and fuller exploitation of existing resources.

The increase in aircraft and personnel continued, rising sucessively from 249 planes and 17,032 men in December 1944 to 287 planes and 19,025 men in January 1945, and then to 332 planes and 22,359 men by July. The Division employed 47,000 civilians as manual laborers and was operating from eight bases in Assam and east Bengal: Chabua, Sookerating, Mohanbari, Misamuri, Tezpur, Jorhat, Shamshernagar, and Tezgaon-Kharagpur having been temporarily taken over by the B-29 project. Traffic problems were eased at the China end of the hump run when the all-weather base at Luliang was opened to extensive ATC traffic. Much time and gas had been wasted by planes stacked up over Kunming and Chanyi, the other two all-weather fields used by ATC. The victory in upper Burma and the destruction of the Japanese air force also made possible the introduction of the C-54 which could use the low hump

Above left: As commander of the India-China Wing, General Thomas Hardin expanded and invigorated the airlift. *Above right:* General William Tunner   pushed the airlift into the 'age of big business'. *Far right:* Indian laborers feed a rock crusher during construction of a new base in India. *Below:* Indian laborers work on an airdrome with B-29s parked in the background

A C-109 is unloaded at Tezgaon
airdrome in India

route and had sufficient range to fly
directly from India to China. This was
another significant step because the
C-54 had a seventy per cent greater
payload than the C-46. In November
1944, operations from Tezgaon in east
Bengal with C-54s and C-109s were
instituted while in January 1945, a
direct C-54 run from Barrackpore near
Calcutta to Kunming was initiated.

To 'produce' a higher aircraft utili-
sation and maintenance, long a problem in the India-China operations,
Tunner introduced Production Line
Maintenance (PLM) which was being
used successfully stateside in Training
Command Bases. PLM required an
aircraft to be towed through a succes-
sion of stations, at each of which a
specially trained crew performed one
specific maintenance operation. PLM
was feasible only if one type of aircraft was assigned to a given base,
hence C-46s were assigned to Chabua,
Sookerating, Mohanbari, and Misamuri; C-87s and C-109s to Jorhat,
Tezpur, and Shamshernagar; and the
new C-54s to Tezgaon. A program of

hangar and apron construction was
also necessary since some bases lacked
hangar and parking facilities.

Tunner had to press his base commanders hard on PLM since there was
some skepticism. Some commanders
feared a temporary loss of efficiency
and hence of tonnage while pilots
questioned the quality of PLM, pre-
ferring each plane to be the responsibility of a given maintenance crew.
Overall, however, PLM was quite
successful. Aircraft in operation rose
from seventy-five per cent in January
1945 to eighty-five per cent in June.
Daily utilization of aircraft at Tezgaon
increased from 7·51 hours in April to
11·65 hours in July. The time required
for the 100 hour inspections of planes
was reduced twenty-five per cent while
the quality of the inspection improved.

Tunner had also still to deal with
one of the most difficult problems of
the airlift, the high mortality rate
of men and planes. Even using the
lower altitude routes, the weather
and terrain of the hump remained a
fearsome problem and exacted a heavy

**C-54s undergo production line
maintenance at Tezgaon**

146

toll of lives and aircraft. The period of January-March 1945 alone saw seventy-seven major accidents and 134 fatalities. The accident rate was causing considerable concern both in the Division and at ATC headquarters in Washington. ATC pressured Tunner who in turn pressed his base commanders, warning, 'In striving for high aircraft utilization, we will *not* sacrifice flying safety. One hour of daily utilization lost can be made up later . . the loss of one load of passengers and crew can never be recovered.' The base commanders were caught between the continuing demands for tonnage and the new insistence on an absolute decrease in accidents. Anxious to raise the tonnage still further, Stratemeyer argued to the ATC commander, General George, that the India-China Division accident rate per flying hours and sorties was low in relation to those of a combat operation. He urged George to consider the hump a combat operation and view accidents from that standpoint. George agreed to measure Division accidents in

terms of hours flown rather than actual numbers but continued his insistence on a higher standard of safety. The base commanders actually satisfied both by increasing tonnage from 44,098 in January to 53,315 in August but lowering accidents and fatalities from twenty-three of the former and thirty-six of the latter in January to eight and eleven in August.

With the dismissal of Stilwell in October 1944, CBI was divided into the India-Burma and China Theaters. As had Stilwell before him, Wedemeyer as commander of the China Theater continued to control cargo assignment for the airlift through an agency called Hump Allocation and Control or Humpalco. Each month the Division gave Humpalco a presumably firm commitment of lift capability for the upcoming month and estimates for subsequent months. Humpalco then assembled the using agencies in China and determined the tonnage to be

An ATC transport flies the true hump route which had a high accident rate

British troops unload a 25-pounder after the capture of Rangoon

allocated to each for the month. Users placed requisitions for specific supplies with the appropriate agencies after which an India-Burma agency called the Hump Regulating Officer or 'Humpreg' received the shipments and controlled the dispatch of cargo and personnel to China.

As the war wound up to its climax in CBI in early 1945, the pressure for more lift increased as consumption of supplies in China reached a new high. To meet the demand, ATC planned to build a fleet of 272 C-54s to replace its C-87s and C-109s which had a 500 per cent higher accident rate than the C-54. The plan failed because ATC could not send enough C-54s to CBI for the Division to carry the required volume of cargo, delivering in April only 44,254 tons of its 48,770-ton quota for the month. Stratemeyer therefore planned yet another augmentation of the airlift. After the capture of Ran-

goon in May, he assigned to the airlift the tactical units of his air force whose primary mission had been completed. This reinforced the hump with the 7th and 308th Bomber Groups, the 443rd Troop Carrier Group, the 3rd and 4th Combat Cargo Groups, and twelve airdrome squadrons. The India-China Division fixed quotas of tonnage, prescribed routes and destinations, and established procedures for dispatching, briefing, air traffic control, loading, and reporting. The new groups were assigned to various ATC bases in India and China.

Stratemeyer's augmentation program brought 261 additional planes to the hump but also brought some problems. These had been combat units which looked down on the hump as a non-combat operation. To them, the assignment was a degrading anticlimax to the war and led to some friction with Division personnel. The units also resented the special training and briefing required for the hump routes. Nevertheless, the tactical

units did make a good contribution to the lift in the summer of 1945, adding 6,488 tons in June, 20,000 in July. and 11,000 in August.

The hump reached its peak in the summer of 1945. At that point, the Division had 330 C-46s, 167 C-47s, and 132 C-54s, not all of which were assigned to the China run. The trans-India service was still maintained by between sixty and seventy planes while a similar number were assigned to an intra-China service which had been set up the preceding fall to help ease the internal supply distribution problems in China. The regular lift over the hump was 58,000 tons in June and reached its high point of 71,042 tons in July. The end of hostilities brought a swift decline, however, as the lift dropped to 53,315 tons in August, 39,775 in September, 8,646 in October, and 1,429 in November, the same month in which the hump was officially closed. Tunner had directed that V-J Day was to be the signal for removing 'the high pressure, daily trip conscious-

Chinese and American soldiers are flown over the hump to China

ness . . . from each operating base The primary mission of the Division was now 'safety and service rather than tonnage'. After V-J Day, therefore, the most dangerous routes were abandoned and other safety measures put into effect. The decline of the east-bound lift caused by the collapse of Japanese resistance was offset some-what by new troop movements within China as the Division received a number of assignments to fly Chinese troops to occupy forward areas. In September, for example, 26,000 Chinese soldiers were airlifted to Shanghai. At the same time, 47,000 Americans were flown west over the hump to India for debarkation.

After reaching its pinnacle, the decline of the hump was as swift as its growth had been slow and painful, a growth which progressed through three phases. From its inception in the spring of 1942 to the summer of

General Stilwell, enjoying a smoke somewhere on the Burma front in February 1944, was a controversial figure in CBI

1943, the airlift was hardly more than a primitive barnstorming operation, struggling to deliver a few thousand tons under near impossible conditions and with hopelessly inadequate resources. This initial non-development of the hump is related to the Allied conception of CBI not as a major arena in the war but as a theater of holding action only. Between the summers of 1943 and 1944 came a year of hardwon expansion aimed at supporting the air offensive in China and the ground offensive in Burma. The expansion also was a key factor in helping the Allies to withstand the great Japanese offensives against Imphal and east China. Finally, after mid-1944, the airlift entered a period of no limits and became the largest and most complex mass transport operation of its time.

At least one key individual can be identified with each of these periods. Although Naiden pioneered the air route and Alexander nursed it through its initial period under ATC, the dominant figure in the early phase has to be Bissell. First as CBI Air Advisor and then as Commander of the Tenth Air Force, Bissell unquestionably helped to mold Stilwell's view that the hump could never move quantities of supplies or be greatly expanded, which may help to explain why the necessity for land communications with China assumed a disproportionate place in his thinking. Bissell seems also to have shared Stilwell's deep distrust of the Chinese leadership as well as some of Stilwell's interpersonal conflicts in the theater, including those with Chiang Kai-shek and Chennault, while adding friction with both CNAC and ATC on his own. While admittedly many other factors held back the growth of the airlift in this period, the negative atmosphere created by Bissell set the tone of the

early phase of the airlift. With his vigor and management innovations, Hardin was the individual most responsible for expanding the lift in 1943-1944 but perhaps one of his most important contributions was to change the general attitude toward the hump from one of limitation to one of dynamic growth and potential. When he was relieved in September 1944, the flight crews of the hump run held a 'Tom Hardin' day in his honor, moving a new record of 1,300 tons in a twenty-four hour period. As the airlift grew into an increasingly large and complex operation, it remained for an executive like Tunner to harness it for unlimited growth and productivity and thus bring the airlift to its final achievement.

Towering above all others, however, is the figure of Stilwell. Throughout the war, Stilwell and his supporters in the War Department, most notably Marshall and Stimson, remained firm in the belief that the possibilities of air supply were limited, hence the

American tanks manned by Chinese crews on the Ledo Road which linked Assam with Myitkyina and the Burma Road

necessity for the north Burma campaign and the Ledo Road. Roosevelt, Arnold, Chennault, and others in the American military as well as the British and Chinese all believed that the road could never be completed in time to move any quantity of supplies, therefore the available resources should instead be allocated solely to the airlift. In retrospect, it would appear that the latter view was closer to reality. Between 1941 and 1945, eighty-one per cent of the tonnage which reached China was airlifted, 16·6 per cent went over the Ledo and Burma Roads (including the weight of the carrying vehicles), and 2·4 per cent went via the Ledo-Myitkyina-Kunming pipeline. Open in January 1945, the Ledo Road suffered a variety of difficulties, including convoys that ran out of gas and had to be

Would China have collapsed without American aid ?

air-supplied and a severe shortage of drivers. Finally, the War Department decided that it would be used only for supplying the Myitkyina area, which had become a major supply depot for the Burma campaign, and that the Burma Road would be used only for the one-way delivery of vehicles and artillery to China. Stilwell's conquest of north Burma, however, was most significant for the relief of China, not in terms of opening ground supply, but rather for the new possibilities it brought to the airlift. Although not a supporter of the airlift, Stilwell did therefore make an important contribution to its development.

Although CNAC has not played a large role in this narrative, ATC owed its neighbor an important debt. It was a CNAC plane which made the first survey flight over the hump in December 1941 just as it was CNAC which began the first service between India and China when all land routes other than the Burma Road had been closed. In the dark days of 1942-1943, it was the example of CNAC which overcame the many doubts about the feasibility of the airlift and kept first the Tenth Air Force and then ATC in business over the hump. CNAC was usually ahead of ATC, such as when it introduced night flying on the hump run, and throughout maintained far more efficient operations. Early recognizing the nature of CNAC, Arnold proposed turning the airlift over to the Chinese-American cooperative but his proposal was firmly vetoed by Stilwell, so CNAC's role in American aid was limited to flying some lend-lease under contract. Stating that he thought it was unessential to the war effort, Bissell also was unsympathetic to CNAC and proposed conscripting its planes and pilots, but such a move was opposed by most knowledgeable Americans and did not come to pass.

A total of 650,000 tons of gasoline, munitions, other supplies, and personnel was flown over the hump, more than half in 1945 alone. Yet this tonnage could have been hauled in seventy liberty ships or 6,500 railroad cars. What end was then served by the extraordinary effort and the lives expended on the airlift? Virtually none of the hump tonnage reached the Chinese people and relatively little reached the Chinese armies engaging the Japanese in China. Much of the tonnage went directly to Chennault while most of the remainder went to special projects such as equipping Chinese troops for the Burma campaign and MATTERHORN, neither of which made much of a direct contribution to the China Theater. Thus the main Chinese resistance to Japan benefited little from the airlifted supplies, although it could be argued that the régime of Chiang Kai-shek would probably have collapsed without the support of Chennault's forces which were wholly dependent on the airlift.

American policy was to keep China from dropping out of the war, at first primarily on the grounds that China was engaging large numbers of Japanese troops and later in a mistaken belief in the military and political contribution China could make. The original premise was certainly the most sound as the facts show. When the Pacific War began in December 1941, China was engaging approximately 1·2 million Japanese troops compared to the 500,000 used in the offensives in the South Pacific and Southeast Asia. Of the 2·3 million Japanese troops overseas at the war's end in 1945, slightly over a million were demobilized in China proper. Thus about half of Japan's overseas troops were contained in China during the war, troops which certainly would have made a significant contribution to Japan's defense in the Pacific had China's collapse permitted their release. Although the Chinese did not strike great military blows against the enemy, and indeed were quite incapable of such blows, China therefore did make its own passive but significant contribution to the Allied cause in the Pacific. To the extent that the airlift helped maintain China

Japanese troops in action. Over a
million of these troops were tied down
in China during the war

in the war for four years, therefore, the effort was worth the price.

As has already been pointed out, the American aid given to the Chinese armies was insignificant in quantity and did not affect the military stalemate between the Chinese and the Japanese until other American activities in the form of the B-29 project, of which the Japanese were well aware, and the offensive of the Fourteenth Air Force galvanized the Japanese into major offensive action in the spring of 1944. Apart from the problem of getting supplies through the blockade, it is doubtful that the Chinese could have used much more lend-lease than they actually did receive. Once delivered, much of the aid was not used effectively, a fact which continuously frustrated Stilwell and the American Military Mission in Chungking. As a result, the War Department steadfastly refused to give the Chinese control of lend-lease on the same basis as the British and Russians, another regular sore point in Sino-American relations during the war.

The conclusion thus arises that the visible fact of American aid may have been more important to keeping China in the war than the actual amount and utilization of such aid. From this perspective, both the hump and Chennault's operations were crucial because they were the two concrete evidences of American support and as such were important political symbols for Chiang's régime. Knowing that China alone could never defeat Japan, Chiang's war strategy had been to hold out until the major powers became embroiled in the war and defeated Japan on other fronts. Thus his needs were not so much military aid to break the military stalemate in China but political, economic, and psychological support to withstand the internal pressures leading to collapse and capitulation.

Many of Chiang's demands for more aid, for control of lend-lease, and for a voice in the Allied councils of war were therefore moves to bolster the political prestige of his régime as well as to secure the specific ends desired. Conversely, every defeat by the enemy and every snub by the Allies cost Chiang dearly in political terms, weakening his image as 'legitimate' leader of China and his position vis-à-vis his internal opponents. The presence of the airlift and the Fourteenth Air Force in China were the two continuing, positive symbols of American support and hence reinforced Chiang's political position and boosted the morale of his armies and people. Without, therefore, reducing either the actual logistic accomplishment of the airlift or the tactical contribution of the Fourteenth Air Force, both of which were considerable, the perspective of time suggests that the moral support provided by each, and perhaps more so in the case of the hump, may have been as important to China's war effort in the long run as the logistic and tactical support.

The Americans in CBI accomplished a number of impossibles: the hump, the Ledo Road, the pipeline to China, the conquest of north Burma, but only the hump had a significance which went beyond the end of the war. The peculiar logistic circumstances under which the Americans tried to break the blockade of China became the birthplace of mass strategic airlift. The India-China Division of ATC proved that a vast quantity of cargo could be air-delivered under the most unfavorable circumstances if the men who controlled the aircraft, terminals, and materials were willing to pay the price in men and money – and the price was high over the hump. As a result of the India-China experience, it was possible to conceive and operate successfully the Berlin airlift in 1948. Two years later, when the outbreak of the Korean War required the emergency delivery of large numbers of troops and equipment to the Far East, the precedents and techniques for such an air movement were already available.

With American aid, Chiang Kai-shek's regime survived nine years of war against the Japanese but lost the postwar struggle with the Chinese communists

Bibliography

Air Force Diary by James H Straubel (ed) (Simon & Schuster, New York)
A History of the World's Airlines by Reg Davies (Oxford University Press, London)
A Military History of Modern China by FF Liu (Princeton University Press, Princeton)
Air Transport at War by Reginald M Cleveland (Harper, New York)
China and the Helping Hand, 1937-1945 by Arthur N Young (Harvard University Press)
Flying Tiger: Chennault of China by Robert L Scott (Doubleday, New York)
Global Mission by HH Arnold (Harper, New York)
Stilwell and the American Experience in China, 1911-1945 by Barbara W Tuchman (MacMillan, New York)
The AAF Against Japan by Vern Haugland (Harper, New York)
The Army Air Forces in World War II by Wesley F Craven and James L Cate (eds) (University of Chicago Press)
The Brereton Diaries by Louis H Brereton (William Morrow, New York)
The China Tangle by Herbert Feis (Atheneum, New York)
The United States Army in World War II: China-Burma-India Theater by Charles F Romanus and Riley Sunderland (Department of the Army, Washington)
Way of a Fighter by Claire L Chennault (Putnam, New York)